IMAGES OF SPORT

SHEFFIELD WEDNESDAY 1867-1967

Yours Sincerely

IMAGES OF SPORT

SHEFFIELD WEDNESDAY 1867-1967

NICK JOHNSON

Frontispiece: Tom Cawley played a key role in helping save Wednesday from the threat of possible extinction in 1887. The Wednesday committee were strongly opposed to the professional game adopted by the FA two years earlier, but Cawley and the likes of Willie Mosforth and Teddy Brayshaw believed that players should be compensated for the loss of time from their employment. A group of players decided to form a new professional club, Sheffield Rovers, forcing Wednesday president John Holmes and his colleagues into a re-think as they faced the prospect of losing important members of the team. After talks between Wednesday chiefs and Mosforth, Cawley urged his team-mates to give the club one last chance. At a special meeting at the Garrick Club on Sycamore Street, Wednesday turned professional on 22 April 1887. The first wages were 5s for home games and 7s 6d for away games.

First published 2003

Tempus Publishing Limited
The Mill, Brimscombe Port,
Stroud, Gloucestershire, GL5 2QG
www.tempus-publishing.com

British Library Cataloguing in Publication Data.
A catalogue record for this book is available from the British Library.

ISBN 0 7524 2720 2

Typesetting and origination by Tempus Publishing Limited.
Printed in Great Britain by Midway Colour Print, Wiltshire.

Contents

The Adelphi pub, which stood on the corner of Arundel Street and Sycamore Street, was the birthplace of 'The Wednesday Football Club' on the evening of 4 September 1867.

The pub was demolished in the late 1960s and the Crucible Theatre was built on the site in 1971. Members of The Wednesday Cricket Club wanted a sporting activity during the winter months. The cricket club had been formed by a group of Sheffield craftsmen who used the 'Wednesday' name as it was the day they regularly took afternoons off to pursue their sporting pastimes. F.S. Chambers (vice-president), John Marsh (secretary) and John Pashley formally proposed the formation of the football club and local businessman Bob Chatterton was the club's first president. The football club overtook the cricket and in 1883 it broke free. The cricket club, which had been in existence since 1820, survived until 1924 when it folded due to a lack of support.

Introduction

This book has been compiled to provide a series of images from the first 100 years of Wednesday's existence. It is not intended to be a comprehensive history of the club: such can be found in previously published books.

The images chart the highs and lows of a club with a proud history. The city of Sheffield led the way in organised football and 'The Wednesday' – as they were originally known – played a prominent role. After turning professional in 1887, Wednesday gained admission to the Football League five years later. They made rapid progress, winning the FA Cup in 1896 and emerging as a leading club.

Further League and Cup success followed after the turn of the century, including back-to-back First Division titles on two occasions. Images of early leading figures like Tom Cawley and Thomas Crawshaw are featured in this book, along with the highly influential Sir Charles Clegg who gained national fame as chairman and president of the FA. Ted Catlin, Ronnie Starling, Redfern Froggatt, Ellis Rimmer and Derek Dooley are among the legendary players also included.

Much of the material has never been published before and I express my gratitude to those listed in the acknowledgements (pg 128) who have loaned items for inclusion.

Why just concentrate on the first 100 years? Well, with the wealth of material available, it was felt that a single book covering the history of the club to date would not do it justice. Also, following relegation to Division Two at the time of writing the book, it would be inappropriate to end on a low point in the club's history.

Here's looking forward to the publication of a second volume when Wednesday's fortunes have improved!

Nick Johnson
September 2003

HRH the Prince of Wales presents the FA Cup to Wednesday captain Ronnie Starling following the victory over West Bromwich Albion at Wembley in 1935.

Wednesday's first 'ground' was on a field where the Highfield library now stands. They subsequently used fields at Myrtle Road, Hunters Bar and Sheaf House. More important games were staged at Bramall Lane.

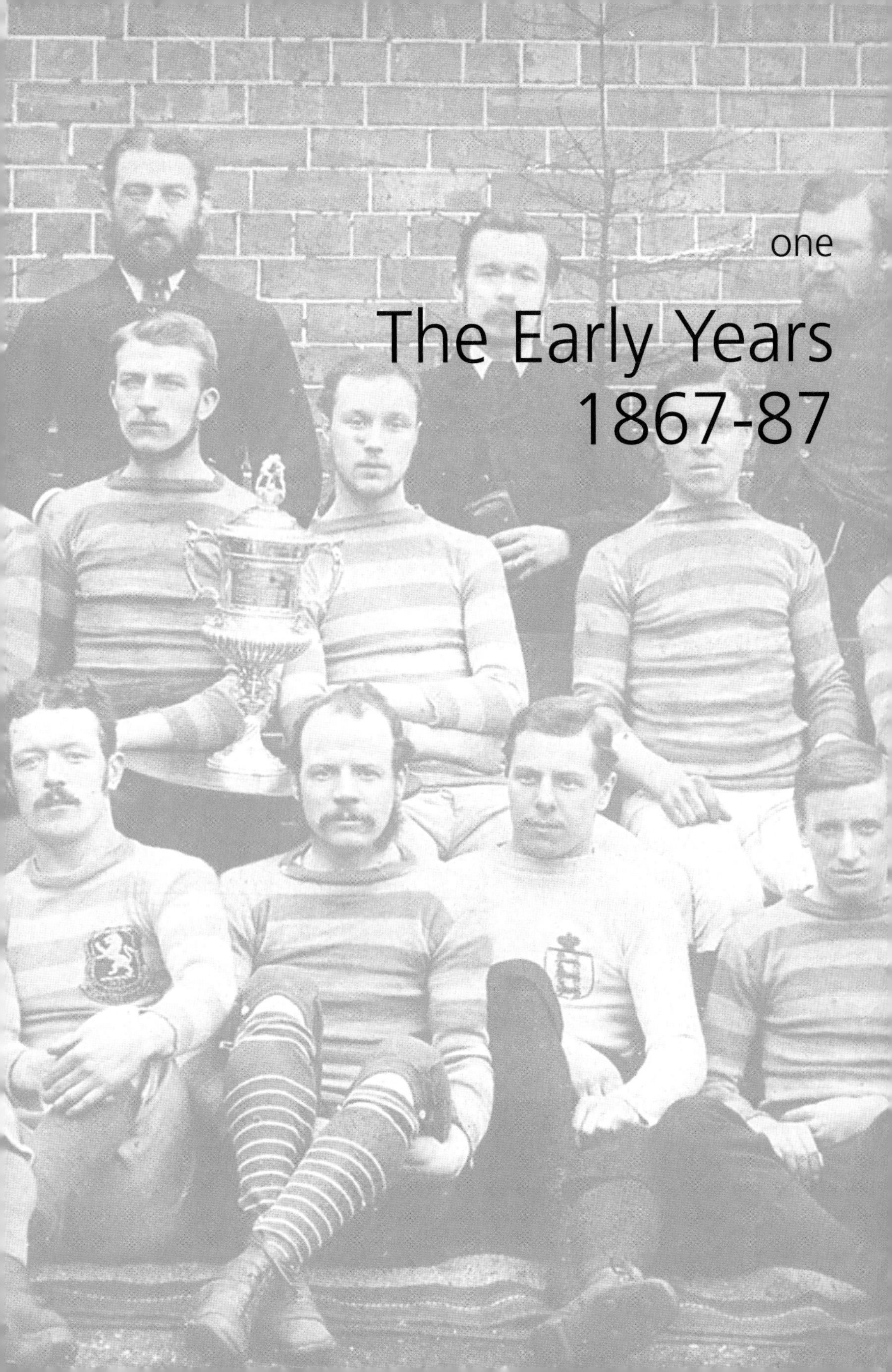

one

The Early Years 1867-87

One of Wednesday's early fixtures was at Dronfield on 31 December 1867; they won the match 1-0. It is recorded that Dronfield scored four 'rouges' – a form of try – while Wednesday scored through the 'inner' posts for a 'proper' goal. Sheffield FC, the oldest football club in the world, are now based in the town at the Coach & Horses Ground.

Left: Wednesday won the Cromwell Cup – put up by Theatre Royal stage manager Oliver Cromwell – beating the Garrick Club 1-0 after extra time in the final at Bramall Lane on 15 February 1868.

Opposite below: Sheffield *v.* Glasgow at Bramall Lane, 11 February 1882. This was a representative team from the Sheffield area, which featured the Wednesday quartet of Mosforth, Wilkinson, Buttery and Hudson. Sheffield won 1-0. From left to right, back row: J.C. Shaw (President), J.R. Harvey (Honorary Secretary), H. Wilkinson (Wednesday), W.E. Clegg (Vice-President), J. Stevens (Pye Bank), J.C. Clegg (umpire), E. Buttery (Wednesday), W.P. Dix (referee). Middle row: J. Hudson (Wednesday), W. Harrison (Redcar), J. Hunter, captain (Heeley), T.E. Cowley (Burton Star), W. Mosforth (Wednesday). Front row: H. Winterbottom (Heeley), A. Mallinson (Barnsley), H.P. Marple (Staveley).

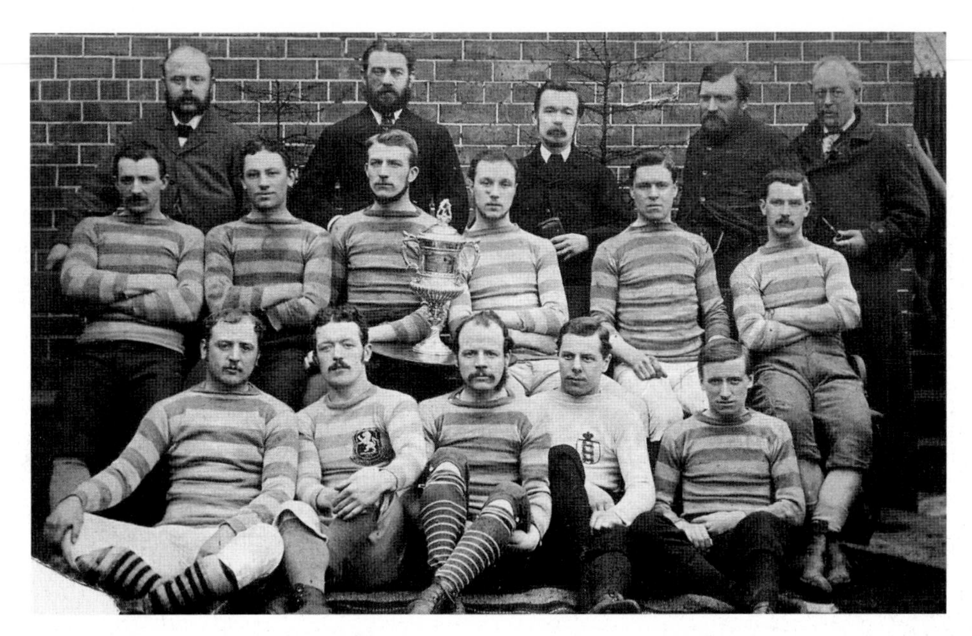

Above: Sheffield Challenge Cup winners, 1881. From left to right, back row: W. Fearnehough, H. Hawksley (President), W. Litttlehales (Secretary), J. Holmes (later President), Anderton (local reporter). Middle row: Charles, Jack Hudson, Bob Gregory, Chas Stratford, Arthur Malpas, Tom Buttery. Front row: Jack Bingley, James Lang, William Stacey, Billy Mosforth, Herbert Newbould. Wednesday won the trophy for the third time after thrashing Ecclesfield 8-1 in the final. Gregory bagged five goals, with Mosforth (2) and Bingley also on target.

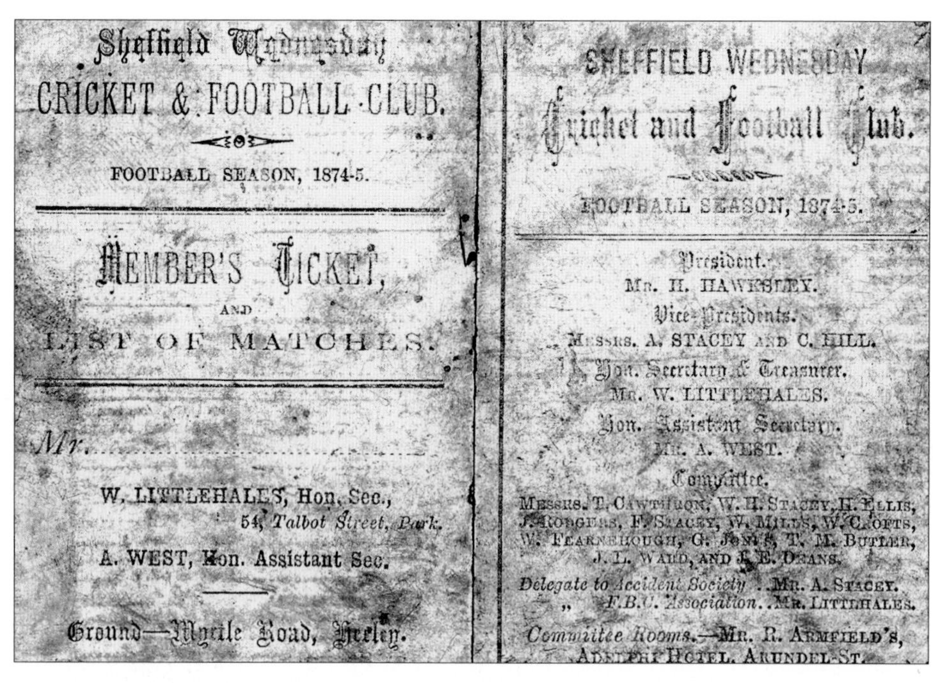

Sheffield Wednesday
CRICKET & FOOTBALL CLUB.
FOOTBALL SEASON, 1874-5.
MEMBER'S TICKET,
AND
LIST OF MATCHES.
Mr. ....
W. LITTLEHALES, Hon. Sec.,
54, *Talbot Street, Park.*
A. WEST, Hon. Assistant Sec.
Ground—Myrtle Road, Heeley.

SHEFFIELD WEDNESDAY
Cricket and Football Club.
FOOTBALL SEASON, 1874-5.
President.
MR. H. HAWKSLEY.
Vice-Presidents.
MESSRS. A. STACEY AND C. HILL.
Hon. Secretary & Treasurer.
MR. W. LITTLEHALES.
Hon. Assistant Secretary.
MR. A. WEST.
Committee.
MESSRS. T. CAWTHORN, W. H. STACEY, H. ELLIS, J. RODGERS, F. STACEY, W. MILLS, W. CROFTS, W. FEARNEHOUGH, G. JONES, T. M. BUTLER, J. L. WARD, AND J. E. DEANS.
Delegate to Accident Society .. MR. A. STACEY.
" *F.B. Association* .. MR. LITTLEHALES.
Committee Rooms.—MR. R. ARMFIELD'S, ADELPHI HOTEL, ARUNDEL-ST.

Above and below: An early fixture card showing Wednesday's programme for the 1874/75 season. Wednesday emerged as the town's leading club within ten years of formation. They won the newly-introduced competitions the Sheffield Challenge Cup (1877) and the Wharncliffe Charity Cup (1879).

LIST OF MATCHES FOR THE SEASON, 1874-5.

Day.		Date.	Against.	Class of Match.	Played at.
Saturday ..	Oct.	3rd	Attercliffe	1st Twelve	Attercliffe ....
Saturday ..		10th	Practice Match	....	Myrtle road.......
Saturday ..		17th	Fir Vale	1st Twelve	Fir Vale ....
Saturday ..		24th	Crystal Palace, Thurlstone	Mixed Fourteen..........	Thurlstone ....
Saturday ..		24th	Broomhall	3rd Fourteen	Myrtle road.......
Saturday ..		31st	Heeley	1st Twelve	Heeley ....
Saturday ..	Nov.	7th	London v.	Sheffield.	Bramall lane .....
Saturday ..		14th	Exchange Brewery	14 v. Ex. Brewery 1st 14 ..	Myrtle road.......
Saturday ..		21st	Norfolk..................	2nd Twelve	Norfolk Park .....
Saturday ..		28th	Norfolk..................	3rd Fourteen	Myrtle road.......
Saturday ..	Dec.	5th	Practice Match	....	Myrtle road.......
Saturday ..		12th	Heeley	2nd Fourteen	Heeley ....
Saturday ..		19th	Royal Engineers	v. Sheffield.	Bramall lane .....
Saturday ..		26th	Broomhall	1st Twelve	Ecclesall road.....
Monday		28th	Broomhall	2nd Fourteen	Ecclesall road.....
Saturday ..	January.	2nd	Sheffield v.	London.	The Oval, London .
Saturday ..		2nd	Norfolk..................	2nd Twelve	Myrtle road.......
Saturday ..		9th	Heeley	2nd Fourteen	Myrtle road.......
Saturday ..		16th	Attercliffe	1st Twelve	Myrtle road.......
Saturday ..		23rd	Derwent	1st Twelve	Sheffield ....
Saturday ..		30th	Crystal Palace, Thurlstone	Mixed Fourteen	Thurlstone ....
Saturday ..		30th	Broomhall	3rd Fourteen	Myrtle road.......
Saturday ..	Feb.	6th	Broomhall	1st Twelve	Myrtle road.......
Saturday ..		13th ...	Exchange Brewery	14 v. Ex. Brewery 1st 14 ..	Rock street ....
Saturday ..		20th	Norfolk	3rd Fourteen	Norfolk Park .....
Saturday ..		27th	Heeley	1st Twelve	Myrtle road.......
Saturday ..	Mar.	6th	Broomhall	2nd Fourteen	Myrtle road.......
Saturday ..		13th	Derwent	1st Twelve	Derby ....
Saturday ..		20th	Fir Vale	1st Twelve	Myrtle road.......

two

Their First FA Cup Win 1887-98

Olive Grove, home to Wednesday from 1887 to 1899. Prior to taking up residence at Olive Grove, Wednesday played at various grounds in Sheffield. These included Bramall Lane (now home to cross-city rivals Sheffield United) which was then principally used for cricket. The Olive Grove site, near Queens Road, was leased from the Duke of Norfolk. A footpath through the field had to be re-routed and a stream was covered over. There were some difficulties in draining the field and around £5,000 was spent converting it into an enclosed ground.

Before dressing rooms were installed at Olive Grove, the players had to change in the nearby Earl of Arundel and Surrey Hotel.

OPENING MATCH at Olive Grove,

MONDAY, SEPTEMBER 12th, 1887.

THE WEDNESDAY v. BLACKBURN ROVERS

BLACKBURN TEAM.

Right Wing. *Goal.* *Left Wing.*

H. Arthur.

Jos. Beverley. **A. Chadwick.**

Jos. Heyes. **John Barton.** **Jas. H. Forrest.**

S. Douglas. **N. Walton.** **R. Rushton.** **L. H. Heyes.** **J. Berisford.**

WEDNESDAY TEAM.

J. Smith.

F. Thompson. **J. Hudson.**

E. Brayshaw. **W. Betts.** **A. Beckett.**

H. Winterbottom. **G. Waller.** **T. E. B. Wilson.** **T. Cawley.** **W. Mosforth.**

Team sheet from the opening fixture at Olive Grove, against Blackburn in September 1887. Billy Mosforth scored the first goal at the ground and Wednesday fought back from 4-1 down to draw 4-4.

Above: FA Cup runners-up, 1890. From left to right, back row: Teddy Brayshaw, Jim Smith, George Waller, Hayden Morley. Middle row: Jack Dungworth, William Ingram, Billy Betts, Tom Cawley, Albert Mumford. Front row: Harry Woolhouse, Mickey Bennett. Wednesday made their first appearance in the final of the FA Cup after beating London Swifts, Accrington Stanley, Notts County and Bolton Wanderers. It proved to be a disappointing experience, however, as they were thrashed 6-1 by Blackburn Rovers at the Kensington Oval.

Opposite: Ambrose Langley was a tough-tackling full-back who established himself as a popular figure after signing from Middlesbrough Ironopolis. He featured in the 1896 FA Cup-winning side and also helped Wednesday win back-to-back League titles. Langley demonstrated his leadership qualities when he took over the captaincy from Jack Earp. After making more than 300 appearances, he was forced into premature retirement following a bad injury.

Above: FA Cup winners, 1896. From left to right, back row: Mr J. Holmes, Thomas Crawshaw, Ambrose Langley, James Jamieson, Bob Petrie, Mr A.J. Dickinson, Mr A. Nixon. Middle row: W. Johnson (trainer), Harry Brandon, Archie Brash, Jack Earp, Harry Davis, Fred Spiksley. Front row: Alec Brady, Lawrie Bell. After losing at the semi-final stage in each of the previous two seasons, Wednesday made their second final appearance in 1896, facing Wolverhampton Wanderers at Crystal Palace. Fred Spiksley gave the Owls an opening minute lead, but then Black capitalised on an error from Thomas Crawshaw to level within ten minutes. However, Spiksley scored again in the eighteenth minute and this proved to be the deciding goal as Wednesday withstood some late pressure to win 2-1. Incidentally, Wolves keeper Tennant did not realise that Spiksley had scored a second goal, as the ball rebounded back onto the pitch. In response to his query at the final whistle, asking when the replay would be, Wednesday skipper Jack Earp said, 'There's no replay old man, we won by two goals to one, as you will see when we take the medals.' Tennant replied, 'You can't have, for only one shot passed me.'

Opposite below: An invitation to a banquet to celebrate the 1896 FA Cup win. The cup was received by captain Jack Earp from Lord Kinnaird. The team received a rapturous reception when they returned to Yorkshire with tens of thousands turning out to welcome them. The brand new trophy was proudly held aloft from the stage of the Empire Theatre.

A jug commemorating the 1896 FA Cup win. The Earl of Wharncliffe, who was on the Wednesday board at that time, was so delighted with the performance in the final that he ordered a number of jugs from Staffordshire Pottery. They were presented to the players, directors and some of the Earl's personal friends.

Wednesday Football Club.
(Winners of the English Cup)

The Committee request the pleasure of

....

to Dinner at the Masonic Hall, Surrey St, Sheffield,
on Wednesday, October 7th.

Your reply on or before Saturday, October 3rd will oblige
A. J. Dickinson, Hon. Sec.
5, Pool Square,
Sheffield.

Dinner 7.30.

MORNING DRESS.

WEDNESDAY

FOOTBALL ✶ CLUB.

DINNER,

TO COMMEMORATE THE

ENGLISH ∴ CUP ∴ VICTORY.

MASONIC HALL, SURREY STREET,

SHEFFIELD.

Wednesday, October 7th, 1896.

PRESIDENT - - - - MR. JOHN HOLMES.

TOAST LIST.

TOAST .... "The Queen." .... THE CHAIRMAN.

TOAST ...... "The Prince and Princess of Wales, and rest of the Royal Family." .. THE CHAIRMAN.

SONG .... "A May Morning." .... *Denza.*
Mr. A. DAWES.

SONG .... "The Tempest." ....
Mr. A. RIDEN.

TOAST .... "The Corporation of Sheffield." ....
Proposer .... Mr. A. HOLMES. *Reply* .... Mr. Ald GAINSFORD.

DUET .... "Comrades, to Arms." .... *Watson.*
Messrs. DAWES & RIDEN.

TOAST .... "The Winning Team" ....
Proposer .... Mr. J. C. CLEGG *Reply* .... Mr. M. J. EARP.

RECITATION ...... "Our Football Club" .... *Hanley.*
Mr. T. HANLEY.

TOAST .... "The Visitors." ....
Proposer .. Mr. GEO. SENIOR. *Reply* Mr. Ald BATTY LANGLEY, M.P. / Mr. J. B. WOSTINHOLM.

SONG .... "Kathleen Mavourneen." .... *Crouch.*
Mr. A. DAWES.

SONG .... "Simon the Cellarer." .... *Hatton.*
Mr. A. RIDEN.

TOAST .... "The Wednesday Football Club." ....
Proposer .... Mr. Ald CLEGG. *Reply* .... Mr. JOHN HOLMES.

DUET .... "The moon hath raised." ...... *Benedict.*
Messrs. DAWES & RIDEN.

RECITATION ...... "Famerly Kalamities." .... *Hanley.*
Mr. T. HANLEY.

TOAST .... "The Press." ....
Proposer .. Mr. A. NIXON. *Reply* .. Messrs. PARTON & STAINTON.

ACCOMPANIST - - - - MR. G. H. DOUGLAS.

Wednesday Football Club.

(WINNERS OF THE ENGLISH CUP.)

DINNER TICKET.

MASONIC HALL, SURREY STREET.

WEDNESDAY, OCTOBER 7TH, 1896.

DINNER, 7-30. **TICKETS, 5s. Each.**

MORNING DRESS. A. J. DICKINSON, Hon. Sec.

J. ROBERTSHAW, TYP., SHEFFIELD.

Invitation and menu for the FA Cup dinner.

three

A Successful Start at their New Home 1898-1925

PROSPECTUS.

In consequence of the Incorporated Wednesday Football Club having to relinquish their ground at Olive Grove, the above Company has been formed for the purpose of providing another suitable ground whereon to continue the old Club. After considerable difficulty, the Company have fortunately been able to acquire a most suitable piece of land on the Penistone Road, near the High Bridge, Owlerton, containing 10 acres, for £5,000. There will be good approaches to the ground from the Penistone Road, and also from Leppings Lane. The Corporation Tramcars will run within 1 minute's walk from the ground, and the present Railway Station at Wadsley Bridge is about 5 minutes' walk from the ground.

The assets of the old Club are considerably in excess of its liabilities. Both assets and liabilities are taken over by the Company.

Each Shareholder will have the right of free admission to the ground, and the holder of Two Shares will also have free admission to the Stand. In each case a Shareholder may be accompanied by a Lady. Similar privileges will attach to further Shares held by the same Shareholder, and are transferable, but no Shareholder will be entitled to sell any admission ticket.

The Directors reserve the power of withholding the above privileges when deemed necessary, on not more than 12 occasions during any year.

In addition to the privileges above mentioned, the Shareholders may receive dividends of 5% per annum out of the profits.

It is intended to lay out the ground for Football, Cricket, Bicycling, and Athletic Sports, and to erect Covered Stands upon the most improved principles.

Having regard to the past honourable career of the Club, and the desire of the Directors that in the future the Club should be even more successful than in the past, the Directors appeal to the public to assist them in providing the necessary capital, and have themselves agreed to subscribe £2,000.

Forms of application may be obtained from the Bankers, and at the Office of the Company.

Above and opposite: To finance the move to Owlerton and meet all the associated costs, the club was reconstituted and a limited liability company formed with shareholders and a board of directors. An original share certificate is shown above. Local industrialist George Senior, who was Lord Mayor in 1901, became the first Wednesday chairman. A total of twenty-two directors were appointed.

The Wednesday Football Club,

LIMITED,

OWLERTON, SHEFFIELD.

Capital, £7,000: 50 Original Shares of £5 each; Present Issue, 675 Shares of £10 each.

Payable 10/- on application, £1 on allotment, and the balance as required.

Directors:

Coun. GEORGE SENIOR, J.P. (Chairman)

THE LORD MAYOR OF SHEFFIELD, Alderman W. E. CLEGG.

Alderman FRANKLIN, J.P., Ex-Mayor of Sheffield.

J. C. CLEGG, Esq.

Coun. THOMAS NIXON, J.P.

,, B. A. FIRTH, J.P.

,, H. HUGHES.

,, J. R. WHEATLEY.

,, A. M. WILSON.

Coun. W. TURNER.

Mr. WM. TASKER.

,, JOHN HOLMES.

,, WALTER FEARNEHOUGH.

,, JOSEPH MASTIN.

,, ARTHUR JOSHUA DICKINSON.

,, HENRY WOOD.

,, HERBERT NIXON.

,, JOSEPH COWLEY.

,, HERBERT NEWBOULD.

Mr. A. G. W. DRONFIELD.

Bankers:

LONDON & YORKSHIRE BANK, Ltd., High-St. and Shalesmoor, Sheffield.

Solicitors:

Messrs. CLEGG & SONS, Figtree Lane, Sheffield.

Honorary Secretary:

Mr. A. J. DICKINSON, 5, Pool Square, Sheffield.

Thomas Crawshaw was a key figure for Wednesday around the turn of the century, featuring in the FA Cup-winning sides of 1896 and 1907. He played for Park Grange, Attercliffe and Heywood Central before joining Wednesday. A pen picture of Crawshaw from the *Famous Footballers* book published in 1896, read: 'A thorough worker always. As a centre half back he is bound to be of use as he plays a good game from first to last and is unselfish to a degree. A good tackler he uses his head cleverly as well, and as he is not yet twenty-three should become even a better all-round player'.

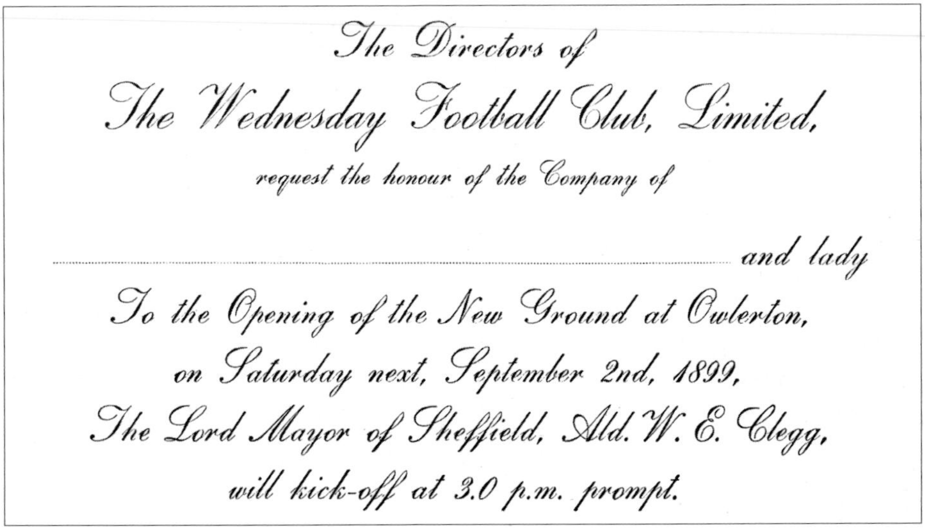

The Directors of

The Wednesday Football Club, Limited,

request the honour of the Company of

.... and lady

To the Opening of the New Ground at Owlerton,

on Saturday next, September 2nd, 1899,

The Lord Mayor of Sheffield, Ald. W. E. Clegg,

will kick-off at 3.0 p.m. prompt.

An invitation to the official opening of Owlerton. Wednesday were forced to leave Olive Grove when their lease expired in 1898. They were unable to renew it because the Midland Railway required the land for track expansion, and they were told to vacate the ground by April 1899. After a period of uncertainty, the club bought a ten-acre site at High Bridge from James Willis Dixon, for the sum of £10,000 plus costs. The new ground was called Owlerton until 1913, when it was changed to Hillsborough. Many people still referred to the ground as Owlerton years later.

THE CITY OF SHEFFIELD

OLIVE GROVE
HOME OF SHEFFIELD WEDNESDAY FOOTBALL CLUB
1887 – 1899
SHEFFIELD WEDNESDAY'S FIRST GROUND AFTER THEY ADOPTED PROFESSIONALISM WAS HERE AT OLIVE GROVE, ON LAND LEASED FROM THE DUKE OF NORFOLK. IN A TWELVE-YEAR STAY THEY EMERGED AS ONE OF THE COUNTRY'S LEADING CLUBS, JOINING THE FOOTBALL LEAGUE IN 1892 AND BRINGING THE FA CUP TO YORKSHIRE FOR THE FIRST TIME IN 1896. WINGER FRED SPIKSLEY-"THE OLIVE GROVE FLYER"-SCORED BOTH GOALS IN THAT 1896 TRIUMPH AND EPITOMISED THE SPIRIT OF AN ERA WHICH ENDED WHEN THIS SITE WAS REQUIRED FOR EXPANSION OF THE MIDLAND RAILWAY LINE.

A plaque marking Wednesday's tenure at Olive Grove is sited on a wall next to a bus shelter on Heeley Bank Road.

Above: An early picture of Owlerton. Wednesday were not unsettled by their move to a new home. In fact, the cross-city switch heralded the start of a very successful era. The first game at Owlerton, on Saturday 2 September 1899, saw Wednesday thrash Chesterfield 5-1, and they lifted the Second Division title that season. Their only home defeat came against Sheffield United who won a bruising FA Cup replay 2-0.

The Wednesday Football Club, Limited

The Directors request the pleasure of the Company of ______________________
to Dinner at the Masonic Hall, Surrey St., Sheffield, on Monday, August 24th 1903, to commemorate the winning of the Football League Championship.

Your reply not later than Wednesday Aug. 19th will oblige

A. J. DICKINSON, Hon. Sec.,

5, Pool Square, Sheffield.

Dinner 7.30. p.m. **Morning Dress.**

Above: An invitation to the 1902/03 Championship celebration dinner. Medals costing £3 apiece were ordered for the players.

.. The .. Wednesday Football .. Club, .. LIMITED.

BANQUET,

. . . AT THE . . .

MASONIC HALL,

On MONDAY, AUGUST 24th. 1903.

TO COMMEMORATE THE WINNING OF THE

LEAGUE CHAMPIONSHIP,

AND THE

MIDLAND LEAGUE CHAMPIONSHIP,

SHEFFIELD CHALLENGE,

AND WHARNCLIFFE CHARITY CUPS.

Chairman ... ... Ald. GEO. SENIOR, J.P.

T. WOODCOCK, SHEFFIELD.

Right: 1902/03 Championship celebration dinner menu.

Opposite: First Division Champions, 1902/03. From left to right, back row: Bob Ferrier, Bill Hemmingfield, Fred Thakeray. Middle row: Davies (assistant trainer), William Layton, Ambrose Langley, Jack Lyall, Thomas Crawshaw, Herrod Ruddlesdin, Frith (trainer). Front row: Vivien Simpson, Harry Davis, Harry Chapman, Andrew Wilson, Jack Malloch, Fred Spiksley, George Simpson. Wednesday held off competition from Aston Villa and Sunderland to land the First Division title for the first time. In a tense finish to the season, Sunderland surprisingly slipped up at Newcastle to hand the trophy to Wednesday. The Owls, who had completed their League programme, were playing in Devon on that crucial day. They added another piece of silverware to their collection by beating Notts County 2-0 to lift the Plymouth Bowl.

First Division Champions, 1903/04. From left to right, back row: Bill Hemmingfield, Jimmy Stewart, Richard Jarvis, William Bartlett. Middle row: Davis (assistant trainer), Bob Ferrier, Ambrose Langley, Jack Lyall, Thomas Crawshaw, William Layton, Henry Burton, Herrod Ruddlesdin, Frith (trainer). Front row: Harry Davis, Harry Chapman, Andrew Wilson, Jack Malloch, George Simpson. Wednesday retained the title after finishing three points clear of Manchester City. They threatened to do the double after progressing to the semi-finals of the FA Cup, but crashed to a 3-0 defeat at the hands of City, who went on to beat Bolton in the final.

The dinner menu from a lavish banquet laid on to celebrate Wednesday's back-to-back title successes. The menu included mock turtle soup and pigeons and beans. Two vocalists, a humourist and a pianist provided the entertainment.

Team group from 1905/06. From left to right, back row: Davis (assistant manager), Tom Brittleton, William Layton, Herrod Ruddlesdin, Thomas Crawshaw, Jack Lyall, Henry Burton, William Bartlett, Frith (trainer). Front row: John Reynolds, Harry Davis, Harry Chapman, Andrew Wilson, Jimmy Stewart, George Simpson, Jack Malloch. Despite producing a strong finish to the season, winning four out of their last six games, Wednesday finished third in the First Division. They also suffered a dramatic 4-3 FA Cup defeat against the eventual winners Everton in the last eight of the competition. The Owls had to settle for the consolation of doing the double over Sheffield United, winning 2-0 away and 1-0 at home. Also that season, Jimmy Stewart became the first Wednesday player to score 20 League goals in a First Division season.

FA Cup winners, 1907. From left to right, back row: A. Dronfield, J. Holmes, A. Dickinson, J.C. Clegg, H. Nixon, J. Thackray, C. Ellis, T. Lee. Middle row: J. Davis (assistant trainer), H. Newbould, Davis, Tom Brittleton, William Layton, Jack Lyall, William Bartlett, Hugh Slavin, Henry Burton, Fred Foxall, P. Frith (trainer). Front row: Frank Bradshaw, Harry Chapman, Andrew Wilson, Thomas Crawshaw, Jimmy Stewart, George Simpson. Wins over Wolves, Southampton, Sunderland, Liverpool and Woolwich Arsenal saw Wednesday book an FA Cup final date with holders Everton. The Owls went into the big game as underdogs, especially as they were below strength, but they won 2-1 with goals from Jimmy Stewart and George Simpson.

Overleaf: 1907 FA Cup banquet menu. The Wednesday players went on a victory parade through the streets of Sheffield with the Corporation band playing 'See The Conquering Hero Comes' and 'Play Up Wednesday Boys' when they reached the Town Hall. The team stepped out onto the balcony and captain Crawshaw lifted the cup in front of an estimated 50,000-strong crowd.

The Wednesday Football Club
LIMITED.

BANQUET

AT THE

Cutlers' Hall,

On FRIDAY, May 17th, 1907.

To Commemorate the Winning of the

Football Association Challenge Cup.

CHAIRMAN—

ALD. GEO. SENIOR, J.P.

Ted Davison punches clear during the 3-2 win at home to Aston Villa on 30 October 1909. The Wednesday players pictured are, from left to right, Davison, Holbem, Bartlett and Spoors.

Simmons scores Sheffield United's second goal in a 3-3 draw at Bramall Lane on 6 November 1909. The Wednesday players shown are, from left to right, Taylor, Spoors and Davison.

Davison punches clear during a 2-0 defeat at home to Everton on 17 December 1910. The other players in the picture are Weir, Warren and Spoors.

Action from the 4-0 defeat at Middlesbrough on 8 January 1910.

Spoors gets in a header during the 1-0 win at Middlesbrough on 7 January 1911.

McLean is thwarted by Bury goalkeeper Raeside during a game at Owlerton on 18 February 1911. Patterson is in close attendance with Wilson pictured in the background.

Walton goes close for Sheffield United in a game at Bramall Lane on 25 February 1911. A goal from McLean gave the Owls a 1-0 win. The players in the photograph are, from left to right, McSkimming, Spoors, Kitchen (United), Peake (United) and Davison.

Opposite above: Wednesday won 2-0 at Newcastle on 14 April 1911 following goals from Wilson and Roberton.

Opposite below: Davison pulls off a save in the 3-1 defeat at Tottenham on 4 September 1911.

RRIS'S
SPORTSMAN

Wednesday avenged their defeat at White Hart Lane earlier in the month with a 4-0 win over Tottenham at Owlerton on 30 September 1911. The scorers were McLean, Burkinshaw, Wilson and Glennon. The players shown in the photograph are, from left to right: Brittleton, Spoors and Davison.

Wednesday under pressure in the annual charity match against Sheffield United at Bramall Lane on 2 October 1911. Players pictured, left to right: Spoors, McSkimming, Kitchen (United), Weir, Davison.

Davison's performance against the Blades is highlighted in this illustration.

Action from the 2-1 defeat at home to Newcastle on 28 October 1911. Players shown, left to right: Campbell, Stewart (Newcastle), Weir, McSkimming, Hibbert (Newcastle).

A Sheffield XI drew 1-1 with a Glasgow XI at Bramall Lane on 21 October 1912. Wednesday duo Davison and Wright feature in the picture.

Ted Davison served Wednesday with distinction for eighteen years. The Gateshead-born goalkeeper joined the Owls in 1908 and went on to make a total of 424 appearances before taking up a player/manager role at Mansfield in 1926. He later had a twenty-year spell as manager of Sheffield United. Davison is in the record books as the shortest keeper to represent England at 5ft 7in, winning his solitary cap against Wales in 1922. He could also lay claim to having discovered Gordon Banks during his second stint as secretary-manager of Chesterfield.

The Wednesday players pictured at the Alexandra Hotel, Saltburn, in January 1912. They trained in the area ahead of their FA Cup first round tie at Middlesbrough. From left to right, back row: Teddy Worrall, Ted Davison, Jimmy Spoors. Middle row: Tom Brittleton, Finlay Weir, Jimmy Campbell, Patrick O'Connell. Front row: Davis (assistant trainer), Sam Kirkman, Ted Glennon, David McLean, Andrew Wilson, George Robertson, Ted Kinnear (trainer).

Team line-up for a game against Chelsea in 1913. From left to right: Ted Glennon, Jimmy Gill, Jimmy Spoors, Bob McSkimming, Tom Brittleton, Teddy Worrall, Jack Burkinshaw, Jimmy Campbell, James Miller, P. Wright, Ted Davison.

Wednesday captain Tom Brittleton with his Middlesbrough counterpart Williamson and referee Heath before kick-off in the FA Cup tie at Ayresome Park on 13 January 1912.

Brittleton and Spoors in the thick of the action in the Cup clash with Middlesbrough. Following a goalless draw at Ayresome Park, Boro won the replay at Owlerton 2-1.

1912/13 team group. From left to right, back row: Davis (assistant trainer), Billy Loyd, Tom Brittleton, Teddy Worral, Ted Davison, Jimmy Spoors, Patrick O'Connell, James Campbell, Ted Kinnear (trainer). Front row: Lawrie Burkinshaw, Sam Kirkman, Ted Glennon, David McLean, Andrew Wilson, George Robertson, P.Wright.

A picture from 1913 showing the construction of the new South Stand. After banking profits of over £5,000 from the 1912/13 season, the Owls board decided to spend on improving the ground. As well as the development of a new South Stand, the Spion Kop was built up at the Penistone Road end.

Workers building the South Stand, which would feature offices, dressing rooms, refreshment areas and a billiards room. It was finally in full use in time for the FA Cup tie against Notts County in January 1914. There were plans to stage an international fixture at the improved stadium the following year, but the outbreak of war forced that idea to be scrapped.

Left: Lacey's shot is saved by Davison during Wednesday's 4-1 win at home to Liverpool on 4 October 1913.

Below: Players in training, *c.* 1913.

Davison saves from Barber in Wednesday's 2-0 defeat at Aston Villa on 11 October 1913. In the photograph, left to right, are Davison, Barber (Villa), Brelsford and Hampton (Villa).

Davison fists the ball away during the game at home to Derby on 1 November 1913. Derby won 3-1 with Spoors netting Wednesday's consolation goal.

Above: The two captains oversee the toss of the coin before Wednesday's FA Cup first round tie at home to Grimsby on 16 January 1913. The Owls advanced to the next round following a comprehensive 5-1 victory, with David McLean grabbing four goals. The powerful Scot went on to hit a hat-trick in the second round replay against Chelsea, after also finding the net in the first game. McLean, signed from Preston in 1911, was a prolific scorer with 100 goals in 147 appearances for Wednesday.

Left: Davison cuts out the danger during the FA Cup first round tie against Notts County on 10 January 1913. Wednesday advanced to the next round following a 3-2 home win. The goalscorers were J. Burkinshaw, L. Burkinshaw and Brittleton.

Right: Best's effort is kept out by Davison in Wednesday's game at home to Sunderland on 29 November 1913. Robertson and Wilson scored in a 2-1 victory.

Tottenham's Walden beats Davison from the penalty spot. Wright was on target for Wednesday in a 1-1 draw at White Hart Lane on 20 December 1913.

On 4 February 1914, during a replayed second round FA Cup tie against Wolves at Hillsborough, a retaining wall at the Penistone Road end of the ground collapsed. The game was stopped while injured fans received medical attention. It was reported that a total of seventy-five people were injured in what was the first recorded accident at a football match in England. Play eventually resumed and Wednesday won 1-0 with Sam Kirkman hitting the winner. The crowd of over 43,000 set a new Hillsborough record.

Opposite: Davison saves from Uttley to help Wednesday beat Sheffield United 2-1 at Hillsborough on 28 February 1914. Glennon and McLean were the goalscorers.

Liverpool go close in a match at Anfield on 7 February 1914. Wednesday won 2-1 with goals from J. Burkinshaw and McLean.

Left: With the wall repaired, Wednesday were able to stage their FA Cup quarter-final against Aston Villa at Hillsborough on 7 March 1914. The record attendance figure was smashed with 57,143 fans turning out to see Villa win 1-0.

Below: Shareholders were invited to view the ground improvements. The new South Stand, which cost £18,000 to build, provided seating for 5,600 and accomodated 3,000 standing supporters.

Wednesday Football Club Limited.

The Directors, being desirous of giving the Shareholders an opportunity of seeing over the New Stand, &c., request the pleasure of the company of .... and Lady at the Wednesday Ground, on the afternoon of Saturday, the 20th of June, 1914, from 3.30 to 5.30.

AFTERNOON TEA.

A. J. Dickinson,
HON. SECRETARY.

Billy Harvey joined Wednesday after the First World War following his demobilisation from the Army. During an FA Cup tie against Darlington in 1920, played in a blizzard, Harvey wore a pair of Corinthian 'knickers' and put his hands in the pockets to keep warm! Harvey was hospitalised after contracting pneumonia while touring with the FA in South Africa. The winger joined Birmingham in 1921 after making 20 appearances for Wednesday.

Wednesday donated £10 10s to sign half-back Oliver Levick from Woodhouse FC in 1919. But he failed to establish himself in the senior side, being limited to 21 appearances before moving to Stockport in 1927.

Twopence.

Souvenir Programme

OF THE

FORTY-FOURTH MATCH

BETWEEN

ENGLAND

AND

SCOTLAND

On the Ground of

THE WEDNESDAY CLUB,

HILLSBOROUGH, SHEFFIELD,

SATURDAY, APRIL 10th, 1920.

KICK OFF 3-30.

Hillsborough was the stage for a full international in 1920 when Wednesday hosted an England *v.* Scotland match. A heavy downpour and unemployment problems in the area saw the fixture attract a lowly 25,536 attendance. But those who turned out were treated to an exciting game as England came back from behind to win 5-4.

George Wilson cost £3,000 – a sizeable fee at that time – from Blackpool in 1920. He was converted from a centre-forward to a centre-half and revelled in his new role, captaining the Owls and winning twelve England caps. But he could not help Wednesday climb out of the Second Division and moved to Third Division (North) side Nelson in 1925 after rejecting a new contract. The timing of the transfer was very unfortunate for Wilson, as Wednesday won the Second Division championship the following season.

THE

WEDNESDAY FOOTBALL CLUB,

LIMITED.

DIRECTORS' REPORT

AND

BALANCE SHEET,

7th MAY, 1921.

Notice is hereby given, that the Twenty-Second Ordinary Annual Meeting of the Company will be held at the Cutlers' Hall, Church Street, Sheffield, on Wednesday, the 29th day of June, 1921, at 7 o'clock in the evening.

The Register of Transfers will be closed from June 18th until after the Meeting.

R. BROWN,
Secretary.

5, Pool Square, Sheffield,
June, 1921.

Loxley Brothers, Ltd., Printers, Fargate, Sheffield.

The balance sheet from 1921. The report stated: 'The Directors have pleasure in submitting the Twenty-Second Annual Report and Accounts and, in doing so, congratulate the Shareholders on a fairly satisfactory season, especially from a financial standpoint. During the year the Club's Debenture Liability has been reduced by the repayment of £2,000'. The freehold land, stands and various fittings were valued at £20,000.

Above: A team group from 1921 before a game against Barnsley.

Left: Billy Powell was a forceful half-back who featured during the 1924/25 season. He lost his place through illness and was unable to force his way back in. Powell left to join Grimsby in 1927.

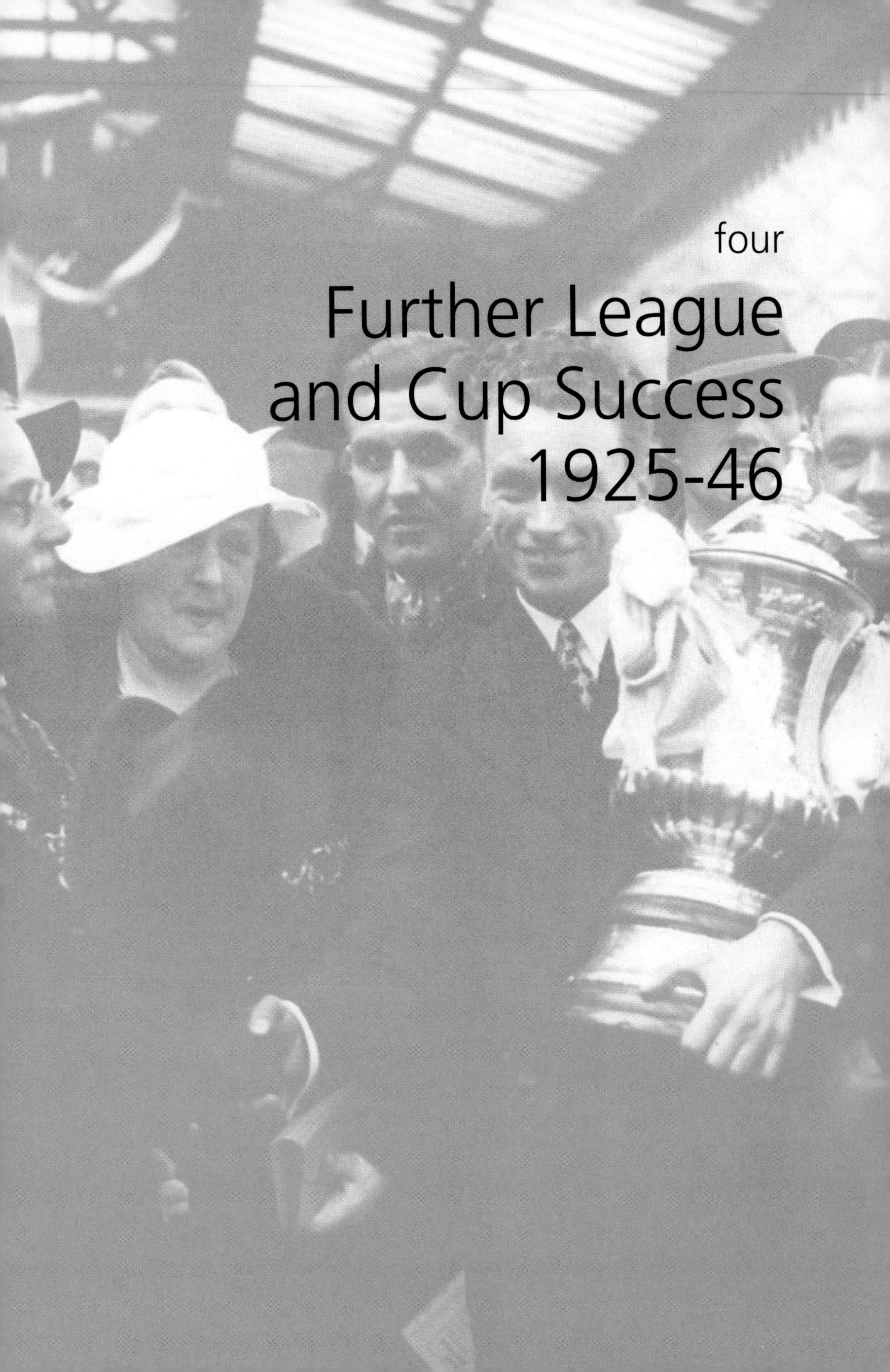

four

Further League and Cup Success 1925-46

Second Division Champions, 1925/26. From left to right, back row: Fred Kean, Arthur Lowdell, Billy Felton, Jack Brown, Frank Froggatt (captain), Ernest Blenkinsop, Billy Marsden. Front row: Rees Williams, Matt Barrass, Jimmy Trotter, Harold Hill, Arthur Prince. Wednesday experienced a dip in fortunes after the end of the First World War before returning to the top flight in 1926. They achieved promotion under Bob Brown who was the club's first professional secretary-manager.

SHEFFIELD WEDNESDAY FOOTBALL CLUB.

Dinner

at the

Royal Victoria Station Hotel, Sheffield,

Friday, 6th August, 1926, at 7 o'clock,

to celebrate the Winning of the 2nd Division League Championship, and of the 60th Anniversary of the Founding of the Club.

SHAREHOLDER. **41** Morning Dress.

1926 Second Division Championship celebration invitation. Promotion was sealed when Jimmy Trotter scored both goals in a 2-1 win at Southampton. The title was secured with a 2-0 home victory over Blackpool on the final day. Trotter, who also scored in that game, set a new club record with 37 League goals, beating the 30-goal haul claimed by David McLean in the 1912/13 campaign.

PROGRAMME.

Toast ... ... THE KING. ... ...

Song ... "Four jolly Sailormen" *German*
Mr. W. H. HANCE.

Toast. THE WEDNESDAY FOOTBALL CLUB.
Proposed by J. McKENNA, Esq.
Response, J. C. CLEGG, Esq., J.P.

Humorous Mr. VINCENT ARTHURS.

Toast ... THE FOOTBALL ASSOCIATION.
Proposed by THE LORD MAYOR (Ald. J Benson)
Response, A. KINGSCOTT, Esq.

Song ... ... "Lorraine" ... *Sanderson*
Mr. JOSEPH GREEN.

PRESENTATIONS by W. G. TURNER, Esq.

Toast ... THE FOOTBALL LEAGUE.
Proposed by Ald. A. J. BLANCHARD, J.P.
Response, CHAS. E. SUTCLIFFE, Esq.

Humorous Mr. VINCENT ARTHURS.

Toast ... CITY AND TRADE OF SHEEFIELD.
Proposed by T. R. ELLIN, Esq:, Master Cutler.
Response, Sir FREDERICK SYKES, M.P.

Song "Devonshire Cream and Cider" *Sanderson*
Mr W. H. HANCE

Toast ... VISITORS and PRESS.
Proposed by A, J. DICKINSON, Esq,
Response (Visitors) HY. KEYS, Esq.
Response (Press) HY. COOPER, Esq.

Song ... "The Sailor's grave" *Sullivan*
Mr. JOSEPH GREEN.

Toast ... THE CHAIRMAN. ... ...
Proposed by F. W. RINDER, Esq.
Response, J. C. CLEGG, Esq., J.P.

SHEFFIELD WEDNESDAY
FOOTBALL CLUB.

DINNER

To celebrate the winning of the 2nd Division League Championship, Season 1925-26, and of the 60th Anniversary of the founding of the Club.

HELD AT THE

ROYAL VICTORIA STATION HOTEL,
SHEFFIELD.

Above: The menu for the Second Division Championship celebration.

HIPPODROME

SHEFFIELD.

TWICE NIGHTLY :-: 6.30 and 8.40.
MATINEES—AS ANNOUNCED.
— ALWAYS BRIGHT AND SELECT. —
Manager: H. C. SAVAGE.

WEDNESDAY v. UNITED.

Played at Hillsboro', Sheffield, Saturday, August 28th, 1926.

THE HIPPODROME

Wednesday.

Right Wing. Left Wing.

Goal.
1 Brown

Backs.
2 Walker 3 Blenkinsop

Half-Backs.
4 Kean 5 Froggatt 6 Burridge

Forwards.
7 Williams 8 Anstiss 9 Trotter 10 Marsden 11 Wilkinson

Referee: Mr. J. W. D. Fowler (Sunderland).

Should any alteration be made, a notice will be sent round giving the name of the substituted player, with the number of the position in which he will play.

Linesmen: Messrs. F. C. Garratt (Nottm.) & C. M. Overton (Lincoln).
(White Flag) (Blue & White Flag)

Forwards.
12 Tunstall 13 Gillespie 14 Johnson 15 Boyle or Hoyland 16 Mercer

Half-Backs.
17 Green 18 King 19 Sampy (T.)

Backs.
20 Birks 21 Harris

Goal.
22 Alderson

Left Wing. Right Wing.

THE HIPPODROME

Right: Wednesday's first game back in the top flight saw them up against the Blades. United won 3-2, with Jimmy Trotter scoring both goals for the Owls. It was the start of a prolific season for Trotter who ended the campaign as the top scorer in Division One with a total of 39 League and cup goals.

First Division Champions 1928/29 and 1929/30. From left to right, back row: Bob Brown (secretary-manager), W.G. Turner (vice-chairman), A. Francis (director), E.G. Flint (director), S.H. Nixon (director), J.B. Gunstone (director), Tony Leach, W. Hopkins (assistant trainer), Jack Brown, A.J. Dickinson (director), Ernest Blenkinsop, W. Fearnehough (director), E. Mills (director), A.J. Blanchard (director), S.P. Stephen (secretary). Middle row: C. Craig (trainer), Alf Strange, Tommy Walker, Sir William Clegg (director), Sir Charles Clegg (chairman), Jack Allen, Ellis Rimmer, W.F. Wardley (director). Front row: Mark Hooper, Billy Marsden, Charlie Wilson, Bob Gregg. Bob Brown transformed Wednesday from a struggling side to Championship winners. In the 1927/28 season they looked certainties for relegation when, with ten games remaining, they found themselves seven points behind their nearest rivals at the bottom of the table. But they enjoyed a superb run, picking up 17 points from a possible 20 to avoid the drop. Jimmy Seed, who had been judged by Tottenham to be past his sell-by date, proved to be an inspirational skipper. The fact that Tottenham were one of the clubs who went down instead of Wednesday must have been a sweet irony to Seed! The Owls landed their first Division One title in a quarter of a century the following season, finishing just a point in front of Leicester. Improved away form the next term saw them retain the title with four games remaining. Runners-up Derby County trailed in ten points behind Wednesday. Jack Allen was the top scorer with 39 goals, beating his tally of 35 the previous year.

Right: Programme from the home game against Arsenal on 7 September 1929. A 2-0 defeat brought an end to Wednesday's impressive run at home. It was the first time a visiting team had won at Hillsborough since February 1928. Wednesday also lost their next home fixture, against Leeds, but then remained unbeaten at Hillsborough for the rest of the season. Incidentally, the name of the club was officially changed from 'The Wednesday Football Club Ltd' to 'Sheffield Wednesday Football Club Limited' in this year.

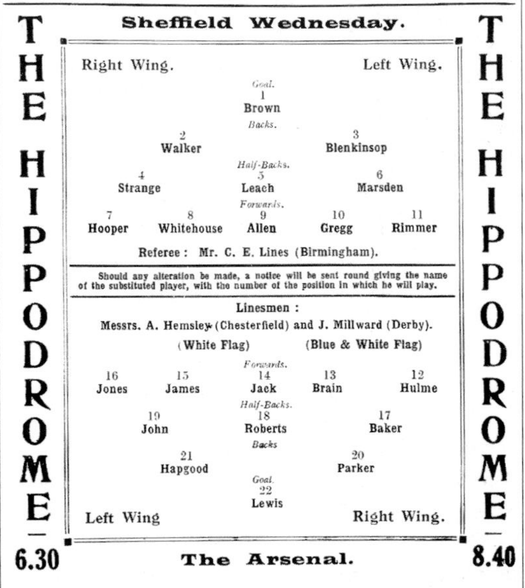

Vol. 30. —PRICE 2d.— No. 2.

THE

HIPPODROME

THE MOST POPULAR SHEFFIELD HALL.

TWICE NIGHTLY :-: 6.30 and 8.40.

THE LATEST, BRIGHTEST and BEST.

Manager: W. B. GIBSON.

Sheffield Wednesday v. The Arsenal,

Played at Hillsborough, Sheffield, SATURDAY, September 7th, 1929.

THE HIPPODROME — 6.30

Sheffield Wednesday.

Right Wing. Left Wing.

Goal.
1
Brown

Backs.
2 Walker 3 Blenkinsop

Half-Backs.
4 Strange 5 Leach 6 Marsden

Forwards.
7 Hooper 8 Whitehouse 9 Allen 10 Gregg 11 Rimmer

Referee: Mr. C. E. Lines (Birmingham).

Should any alteration be made, a notice will be sent round giving the name of the substituted player, with the number of the position in which he will play.

Linesmen:
Messrs. A. Hemsley (Chesterfield) and J. Millward (Derby).
(White Flag) (Blue & White Flag)

Forwards.
16 Jones 15 James 14 Jack 13 Brain 12 Hulme

Half-Backs.
19 John 18 Roberts 17 Baker

Backs
21 Hapgood 20 Parker

Goal.
22
Lewis

Left Wing Right Wing.

The Arsenal.

THE HIPPODROME — 8.40

Above: An England cap awarded to Alf Strange following his appearance against Scotland at Wembley on 5 April 1930. Strange was an inside-forward when he arrived at Hillsborough from Port Vale in 1927, but he did not realise his full potential until switching to wing-half, winning many admirers with his creative play. Strange featured prominently when Wednesday won successive First Division titles in the 1928/29 and 1929/30 seasons, missing just one game. He made 272 appearances and was capped 20 times before moving to Bradford in 1935.

Right: Harry Burgess proved to be an astute signing from Stockport in 1929. He finished second top scorer behind Jack Allen with 19 goals in his first season, helping Wednesday retain the League title. His impressive form in front of goal resulted in him receiving a call-up to the England squad and he won the first of four caps at Bramall Lane in a game against Ireland. After scoring 77 goals in 234 appearances for the Owls, Burgess was sold to Chelsea in 1935.

Opposite: Mark Hooper was a small outside-right who was signed by Bob Brown for £2,000 from Darlington in 1927. He became an automatic choice, making 189 consecutive League and cup appearances. With Ellis Rimmer on the opposite flank, Wednesday boasted what many observers felt to be the best pair of wingers in club football at that time. Hooper secured his place in Wednesday folklore with a goal in the 1935 FA Cup final. He made more than 400 appearances before moving across South Yorkshire to join Rotherham as a coach.

Right above: Sir William Clegg was a Wednesday director for thirty-three years until his death in 1932. Like his elder brother Charles, William was an outstanding athlete who used his speed to great effect playing football. As a solicitor with the family firm, Clegg was defending the notorious Sheffield murderer Charlie Peace when he received a call-up to play for England against Wales in 1879. After preparing evidence for the trial, he travelled to The Oval on the day of the game and his train was delayed by heavy snow. He was allowed to join the action despite arriving 20 minutes after kick-off! Incidentally, Clegg avoided heading the ball – a tactic introduced in Sheffield: 'I tried it once, but my head wouldn't stand it,' he once remarked. After hanging up his boots to concentrate on politics Sir William became Lord Mayor of Sheffield and was dubbed 'The Uncrowned King of Sheffield'.

Right below: Itinerary for an FA XI *v.* Sheffield XI match at Hillsborough in 1931. The match was arranged as a benefit for Wednesday player Billy Marsden who was forced to retire after being injured while playing for England. Marsden received £700 in compensation and Wednesday were paid £2,000. The itinerary included the following instructions: 'Players are required to provide themselves with DARK knickers. White shirts will be supplied. The Players of both teams will "feed" together at the conclusion of the match.'

Marsden Trust Fund Match.

F.A. XI.

(Canadian Tour Players)

V.

A Combined XI. of

SHEFFIELD

(Wednesday & United F.C's.)

To be played on the Ground of the

SHEFFIELD WEDNESDAY F.C.,

Hillsborough, Sheffield,

On MONDAY, 28th SEPT., 1931.

Kick-off 5.30 o'clock.

SHEFFIELD WEDNESDAY FOOTBALL CLUB

Official Souvenir Handbook

For Season 1933-34

RECORD OF ACHIEVEMENTS
PLAYERS :: FIXTURES
LEAGUE TABLES
&c.

Compiled by the

SHEFFIELD WEDNESDAY SUPPORTERS CLUB

Left: Official handbook from the 1933/34 season. Chairman W.G. Turner issued a rallying call to supporters club members: 'No club has a more loyal band of followers than the good old Wednesday, and my regret is that the stress of the times has kept many away from our matches who would have liked to attend. The lean times are passing! Your directors have provided a good team, good sport, cheap season tickets, and fine accomodation, and they and the team are imbued with one idea – to maintain the high reputation that the Wednesday Club has established for good, clean sport. Roll up at home, and let us hear the old Wednesday roar!'

Below: Billy Walker (secretary-manager) with W.G. Turner (chairman) addressing the supporters club members in 1935. Walker was appointed after St Johnstone manager Tom Muirhead failed to secure his release from the Scottish club. During his time in charge, he tried unsuccessfully to bring Stanley Matthews and Tommy Lawton to Hillsborough. Walker's finest hour was leading Wednesday to FA Cup success in 1935. After relegation to the Second Division two years later, the Owls were struggling at the start of the 1937/38 season and Walker resigned following a stormy meeting with shareholders.

Jack Brown, shown here in action during the 1935 FA Cup final, quit his job at Manton Colliery in 1923 to join Wednesday from Worksop Town. He had to wait a few years before taking over in goal from Ted Davison, but eventually made the position his own and helped Wednesday win two League titles and the FA Cup. His efforts were also rewarded with international recognition, winning six England caps. After notching up 507 appearances in 14 years at Hillsborough, Brown left to join Hartlepool.

Above: Jack Palethorpe on the attack against Arsenal at Highbury, on 2 February 1935. Arsenal won 4-1 with Palethorpe scoring Wednesday's consolation. Palethorpe made a useful contribution during his brief spell in Sheffield. Signed from Preston in December 1934, he was with Wednesday for just eleven months before being sold to Aston Villa. But he played a key role in the 1935 FA Cup win, scoring three goals on the way to the final and giving the Owls an early lead at Wembley.

Left: Catlin and Nibloe keep Arsenal's Drake at bay in the 1935 game at Highbury.

Brown clears the danger as Nibloe (on the ground) and Millership look on. Arsenal won 4-1 with the great Alex James grabbing a hat-trick.

Cup training at Cleveleys in 1935.

SATURDAY
27th April

Leave for London.

Sheffield (Midland) depart 8.57 a.m.

St. Pancras arrive 12.8 p.m.

Motor Coaches on arrival at St. Pancras to convey party to Hotel Russell for Lunch at approximately 12.15 p.m.

Motor Coaches leave Hotel for Wembley Stadium at 1.0 o'clock.

Cup Final. Kick-off 3.0 p.m.

Motor Coaches will leave Wembley Stadium immediately after the match to convey Officials and Friends to Hotel Russell.

Motor Coach to convey the Players will leave the Stadium at approximately 5.15 p.m.

Banquet at Hotel Russell at 7.30 p.m. for 8.0 p.m.

SUNDAY
28th April

Breakfast 9.0 a.m.

Motor Coaches will leave Hotel for Brighton at 10.0 a.m. prompt.

Royal Albion Hotel, Brighton, for Lunch. Arrive 1.0 p.m.

Free Afternoon in Brighton.

Tea at Royal Albion Hotel at 5.0 p.m.

Motor Coaches will leave Brighton for Hotel Russell at 6.0 p.m.

Dinner on arrival at Hotel Russell.

MONDAY
29th April

Breakfast 9.0 to 9.30 a.m.

Free morning.

London (St. Pancras) dep. 12.0 noon.

Sheffield (Midland) arrive 3.7 p.m.

Lunch on train.

Cup final itinerary.

Cup final cartoon.

Opposite below: The players at St Pancras station ahead of the 1935 FA Cup final. Wednesday beat Oldham, Wolves, Norwich, Arsenal, Burnley and West Brom on their way to Wembley. Ellis Rimmer had the distinction of scoring in every round of the competition.

Left: An enthusiastic fan waves his rattle before the Cup final. Note the cardboard scissors to mark Sheffield's association with steel.

Below: Cup final team introduced to the Prince of Wales.

Opposite: Existing programmes from the 1935 FA Cup final are usually creased because it was raining that day and fans folded them to fit in their pockets.

PLAN OF THE FIELD OF PLAY
SHEFFIELD WEDNESDAY
Colours: White Shirts and Dark Knickers
(1) Goalkeeper BROWN
(2) Right Back NIBLOE
(3) Left Back CATLIN
(4) Right Half-Back SHARP
(5) Centre Half-Back MILLERSHIP
(6) Left Half-Back BURROWS
(7) Outside Right HOOPER
(8) Inside Right SURTEES
(9) Centre Forward PALETHORPE
(10) Inside Left STARLING (CAPT.)
(11) Outside Left RIMMER
(12) Outside Left BOYES
(13) Inside Left SANDFORD
(14) Centre Forward RICHARDSON (W. G.)
(15) Inside Right CARTER
(16) Outside Right GLIDDEN (CAPT.)
(17) Left Half-Back EDWARDS
(18) Centre Half-Back RICHARDSON (W.)
(19) Right Half-Back MURPHY
(20) Left Back TRENTHAM
(21) Right Back SHAW
(22) Goalkeeper PEARSON
Should the Match result in a draw after ninety minutes' play an extra half-hour will be played
WEST BROMWICH ALBION
Colours: Blue Shirts and White Knickers
Referee: A. E. FOGG (Lancashire)
Linesmen: L. E. GIBBS (Berks and Bucks) A. H. LEPPARD (Surrey)

SATURDAY
APRIL 27, 1935
EMPIRE STADIUM, WEMBLEY
Managing Director — — A. J. ELVIN
FINAL TIE
of
The Football Association Challenge Cup Competition
SHEFFIELD WEDNESDAY
v.
WEST BROMWICH ALBION
Printed and Published by
Fleetway Press(1930)Ltd., 11/21, Emerald St., London, W.C.1
Official Programme Sole Concessionaires

Ellis Rimmer, shown in action during the 1935 FA Cup final, appeared over 400 times for Wednesday and scored 140 goals. Signed from Tranmere in 1928, Rimmer helped the Owls land two successive First Division titles as well as the FA Cup. The winger's impressive form was rewarded with four England caps. Rimmer ended his ten-year association with Wednesday when he left to join Ipswich in 1938.

Jack Palethorpe (wearing white shirt, near penalty spot) fires Wednesday into the lead after just two minutes at Wembley.

Cup final celebration.

Ronnie Starling pictured with the FA Cup at Sheffield's Midland station as the Wednesday players return home.

Opposite: Defender Ted Catlin made over 300 appearances during a fifteen-year career with Wednesday. He made the left-back position his own after succeeding Ernest Blenkinsop and was a member of the 1935 FA Cup-winning team. Catlin was also a pre-war England international, winning five caps. After fighting his way back from a serious injury, he retired in 1945 after losing his place to Hugh Swift. Catlin failed to score in 227 appearances.

Sir Charles Clegg was a hugely influential figure in English football. As chairman of the FA from 1890 until his death in 1937, he played a major role in helping to shape the rules of the game. He and his brother William played for several teams, including Sheffield Albion, before joining Wednesday in 1870. They left to play for other teams, including Sheffield Club and Sheffield Perseverance, because Wednesday's success had apparently become monotonous! Clegg featured in the very first international fixture, a goalless draw between England and Scotland in 1872. He called his team-mates 'snobs from the south', claiming they refused to pass the ball to him and would not talk to him after the match! Clegg became chairman of Wednesday in 1915. As well as being chairman of the FA, he also took on the role of president in 1923.

Sheffield Wednesday Football Club, Ltd.

The Directors request your presence at the Board Room, Wednesday Ground, Hillsbro' on Saturday next, 19th March, 1938, at 2 p.m. on the occasion of the Unveiling of the Memorial to Sir Charles Clegg, J.P. late President of the Club.

R.S.V.P.

J. McMULLAN, Sec-Manager.

An invitation to a memorial function for Sir Charles Clegg following his death in 1937. Clegg's autocratic style led to him being nicknamed 'The Napoleon of Football'. He insisted on fair play and was fond of saying 'no man ever got lost on a straight road'. In a truly remarkable career, Clegg was chairman of Sheffield United at the same time as holding down the same position with Wednesday! He also refereed the 1882 FA Cup final between Old Etonians and Blackburn Rovers.

Defender Albert Ashley was brought to Hillsborough from Mansfield by Billy Walker in 1935, a few months after the FA Cup success. Ashley made only a handful of appearances in his first season at the club, and then found himself frozen out of the side at the start of the 1936/37 campaign. But he went on to become a regular in the side and missed only one game in the 1938/39 season when Wednesday lost out to Sheffield United by a single point in the Second Division promotion race.

The Directors of the
Sheffield Wednesday and Sheffield United Football Clubs
request the pleasure of the company of

....

at the

SHEFFIELD WEDNESDAY v. SHEFFIELD UNITED

Football Match, to be played at the
WEDNESDAY GROUND,
SATURDAY, 16th OCTOBER, 1937
Kick-off 3 o'clock
on the occasion of the visit of the
OFFICERS AND MEN OF H.M.S. "SHEFFIELD"

W. H. Walker,
Wednesday Ground,
Hillsboro', Sheffield 6.

R.S.V.P.

An invitation to the derby clash with Sheffield United in October 1937, which was watched by a crowd of 50,000 and broadcast live across the British Empire. The Blades came out on top, winning 1-0.

Dubliner Bill Fallon had the unenviable task of replacing wing wizard Ellis Rimmer in the team. The Eire international was a regular in the 1938/39 season, scoring 10 goals in 34 appearances. But he played in only a handful of games after that and switched to Notts County in 1946.

Inside-forward Charlie Napier joined Wednesday from Derby in 1938 and helped them emerge as Second Division promotion challengers. He was handed the captaincy by Jimmy McMullan and many feel he would have led the Owls into the First Division had it not been for the war. Towards the end of his Wednesday career, Napier was banned *sine die* by the FA following an incident in a game against Grimsby. The ban was later lifted and he returned to his native Falkirk in 1945. Napier scored 10 goals in 56 appearances for Wednesday.

Goalkeeper Derek Goodfellow's Wednesday career spanned eleven years, including wartime football. He moved to Middlesbrough in 1947 after making 77 appearances.

Douglas Hunt has a place in the record books as the only Owls player to score six goals in a game. He achieved the feat in the 7-0 home win over Norwich City on 19 November 1938. Wednesday turned to Hunt when they were lacking in firepower, spending £3,000 to prise him away from neighbouring Barnsley in March 1938. The fee proved to be a sound investment as his goals helped them avoid relegation from Division Two. Hunt's appearances were limited during wartime and he left to join Leyton Orient in 1946 after scoring 31 goals in 47 games.

Horace Burrows joined Wednesday in the summer of 1931 following stints at Coventry City and Mansfield Town. After taking nearly two years to establish himself as a first-team regular, he then embarked on a run of 136 consecutive appearances. Burrows was a classy half-back who featured in the 1935 FA Cup-winning side. Capped three times by England, he made 260 appearances for Wednesday before retiring in 1942.

OFFICIAL HANDBOOK
OF THE
Sheffield Wednesday
F. C.

SEASON 1939-40.

Pashley & Trickett, Ltd.
Stevonson Rd.,
Sheffield

IRON, STEEL & NON-FERROUS
MANUFACTURERS &
MERCHANTS.

SPECIALISTS
in
Mild Steel Re-inforcing Concrete Bars.
DISMANTLING
of Plant, Machinery and Works.
BUYERS
of all grades of Iron & Steel Scrap.
'Grams : PET. Tel. 41136-7.

Printed and Published by—Hearn's Advertising Service, Ltd., 2 Bridge Road, Willesden, N.W.10

Left: Official handbook for the 1939/40 season. Supporters were tempted with the offer of 'Whist Drives every Tuesday at 8pm during the Football Season in the tea room under the New Stand'.

Below: 1942/43 team group. From left to right, back row: Dave Russell, Walter Millership, Albert Ashley, Albert Morton, Ted Catlin, Joseph Cockroft. Front row: Wally Reynolds, Jackie Robinson, Frank Melling, Jack Thompson, Hugh Swift. Secretary-manager Eric Taylor, who took over control of the team from Jimmy McMullan, guided Wednesday to the League North War Cup final in his first season. They finished third in the Football League (North).

Jackie Robinson was a quick, skilful player who is rated by many as one of the finest inside-forwards to have played for Wednesday. He was particularly effective in the war years, scoring 90 goals in little more than 100 games. His 35-goal haul in the 1942/43 season included no less than six hat-tricks. Robinson went on to play four times for England, scoring on his debut against Finland. He was sold to Sunderland for £7,500 in 1946. Bizarrely, the fee was later reduced when it emerged that Robinson was two years older than people thought!

Action from the second leg of the 1943 League North War Cup final against Blackpool. Reynolds, Robinson and Melling are the players in the picture. Wednesday lost 4-3 on aggregate. After a 2-2 draw in the first leg, a crowd of over 47,000 watched the return match at Hillsborough, when Blackpool won 2-1 with Jackie Robinson scoring Wednesday's consolation.

Opposite below: Redfern Froggatt, Jack Lindsay and Alf Rodgers pictured in 1945. The signing of Lindsay from Scottish club Morton was nearly hijacked in unusual circumstances. There was much interest in the player and attempts were apparently made by 'several unknown individuals' to force him to miss the train taking him from Glasgow to Yorkshire! But he made the trip, scored twice in Wednesday's 4-3 defeat at Leeds and was promptly signed after the match.

Programme from the Royal Air Force *v.* Scotland match at Hillsborough in 1944. Matt Busby featured in the Scotland line-up, while the Royal Air Force side included Stanley Matthews, Ted Drake, Stan Mortensen and Raich Carter. Scotland won 7-1. The programme editorial described the mood of the nation as the end of the Second World War approached: 'The war years have been grim, but sport, and football in particular, have contributed not a little to provide valuable spells of relaxation from the heavy strain and maintain the nation's morale.'

OFFICIAL PROGRAMME

War Charities
Representative Football Match

Sheffield Wednesday Ground

Saturday, 25th November, 1944
KICK-OFF 3 p.m.

ROYAL AIR FORCE
VERSUS
SCOTLAND

PRICE ONE PENNY

1945/46 line-up. From left to right: Jackie Robinson, Cyril Turton, Bill Pickering, Tom Gale, Jack Lindsay, Alex Wands, Derek Goodfellow, Tommy Ward, Redfern Froggatt, Hugh Swift, Charlie Tomlinson. Wednesday switched briefly from their familiar stripes to play in hooped shirts. They had used hoops in early strips, as shown in the opening chapter. Jackie Robinson scored an impressive 17 goals in 21 appearances as Wednesday finished fifth in the Football League (North).

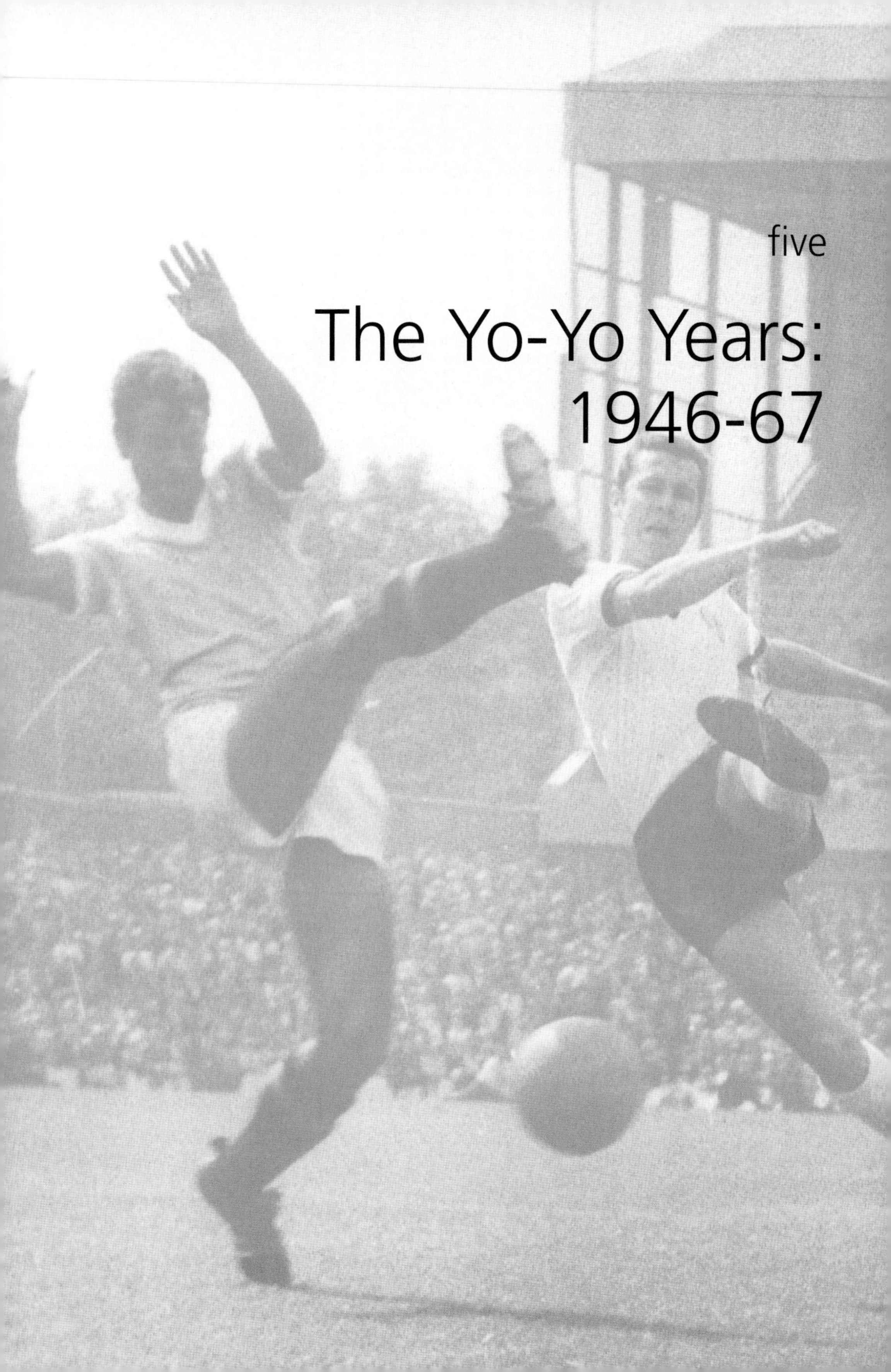

five

The Yo-Yo Years: 1946-67

Eric Taylor pictured in 1947. Taylor earned a reputation as one of the best administrators of his generation and his vision saw Hillsborough develop into a popular venue for FA Cup semi-finals and representative games. He loyally served the club for almost 45 years after arriving as an office boy in 1929. Despite not having played professional football, he enjoyed a sixteen-year spell in charge of team affairs and guided Wednesday to two Second Division titles. He later returned to an administrative role when he was appointed general manager and secretary.

1946/47 team group. From left to right, back row: Sam Powell (trainer), Billy Knox, Douglas Witcomb, Cyril Turton, Francis Westlake, Albert Morton, Hugh Swift, Joseph Cockroft, Eric Taylor. Front row: Frank Slynn, Arnold Lowes, James Dailey, Redfern Froggatt, Dennis Woodhead. Wednesday flirted with relegation to the Third Division (North), losing more than half their games as Eric Taylor struggled to find a winning formula.

Above: A group of players pictured after landing in the Isle of Man at the end of the 1947/48 season. Wednesday's game against Sheffield United in Douglas was the Isle of Man's first game between Football League clubs. Eddie Quigley scored both Wednesday goals in a 2-2 draw watched by a crowd of 8,000.

Left: Eric Taylor landed Clarrie Jordan from South Yorkshire neighbours Doncaster in 1948, paying £6,000 for the centre-forward. Arnold Lowes moved the other way in part-exchange. A former miner, Jordan had been a profilic goalscorer during his time at Belle Vue, but his spell at Hillsborough was blighted by injury problems and he failed to really hit the heights. He retired in 1955 at the age of 33 after scoring 36 goals in 94 appearances.

Above: 1948/49 team group. From left to right, back row: Douglas Witcomb, Frank Westlake, Dave McIntosh, Hugh Swift, Cyril Turton, Joe Cockroft. Front row: Oscar Fox, Eddie Quigley, Clarrie Jordan, Redfern Froggatt, Dennis Woodhead.

Right: Charlie Tomlinson scored the fastest League goal for Wednesday when he found the back of the net just twelve seconds into the game at Preston in October 1949. Initially rejected by Wednesday after joining the club from school, Tomlinson returned to Hillsborough in 1944 at a cost of £1,000 from Bradford Park Avenue. He scored 12 goals in 77 appearances before leaving to join Rotherham in 1951.

Left: Eric Taylor's decision to pay Bury £12,000 for Eddie Quigley in 1947 paid handsome dividends. Quigley was a free-scoring centre-forward who scored 52 goals in 78 appearances for Wednesday. His record is all the more remarkable given the fact he had actually started out as a full-back before switching to the forward line during his time at Bury. When Quigley left to sign for Preston in December 1949, he commanded a British record transfer fee of £26,500.

Below: Players training in 1949, from left to right: Dave McIntosh, Frank Westlake, Kenny Turton and Joe Locherty.

Second Division runners-up, 1949/50. From left to right, back row: Eddie Gannon, Vin Kenny, David McIntosh, Edgar Packard, Hugh Swift, Douglas Witcomb. Front row: Walter Rickett, Alf Rogers, Clarrie Jordan, Redfern Froggatt, Charlie Tomlinson. Wednesday clinched promotion by the narrowest of margins – 0.008 of a goal to be exact – after being held to a goalless draw in their final game at home to Tottenham. They edged out arch-rivals Sheffield United and Southampton, who both finished with the same points tally. Wednesday enjoyed further success after the completion of the League programme, beating the Blades 2-1 at Hillsborough in the County Cup final, with Hugh McJarrow netting a last-minute winner.

FOOTBALL LEAGUE DIVISION II

SHEFFIELD WEDNESDAY

versus

GRIMSBY TOWN

At Wednesday Ground, Hillsborough, Wednesday, 26th April, 1950

Kick-off 6.30 p.m.

Wednesday v. Barnsley   Photo by Sheffield Telegraph & Star

2d.   OFFICIAL PROGRAMME   2d.

Above: From left to right: Eddie Gannon, Edgar Packard and Douglas Witcomb in 1950. Gannon, from Dublin, was an attacking wing-half who was signed from Notts County for £15,000 the previous year. He made over 200 appearances before leaving to become player-manager of Shelbourne in 1955. Packard, who arrived from Clipstone in 1936, had to wait ten years to make his League debut. He was an ever-present during the 1949/50 promotion season and made a total of 126 appearances before joining Halifax in 1952. Witcomb was signed for £6,000 from West Brom in 1947. After 230 appearances for Wednesday, the Wales international wing-half was transferred to Newport in 1953.

Left: Programme from Wednesday's game against Grimsby, 1950.

Right: Walter Rickett was a diminutive winger who could play on either flank. He began his career with Sheffield United in the war years and actually scored with his first touch in senior football – against Wednesday! After a spell at Blackpool, he returned to Sheffield to sign for Wednesday in 1949 at a cost of £6,000. Rickett featured regularly in the 1951/52 Second Division Championship-winning side, but he was sold to South Yorkshire neighbours Rotherham soon afterwards. His record for the Owls was 13 goals in 97 appearances.

Below: Dennis Woodhead, seen here on the treatment table, was primarily an outside-left, but he featured as an emergency centre-forward on occasion and chipped in with his fair share of goals. His most fruitful spell was in the 1953/54 season when he scored 21 times in 45 games, helping Wednesday reach the semi-finals of the FA Cup. His overall record was 76 goals in 226 appearances before he made the short move to Chesterfield in 1955 following Wednesday's relegation to Division Two. Woodhead returned to Hillsborough in 1971, succeeding Derek Dooley as the Development Officer on the commercial side and spending a further sixteen years at the club.

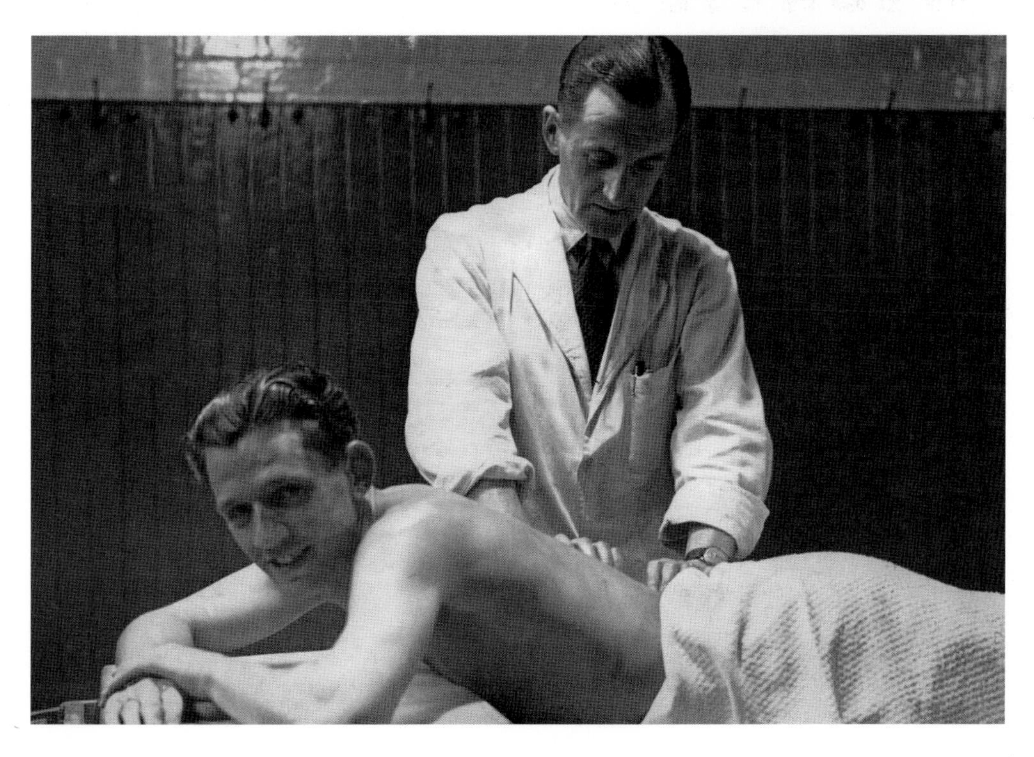

Above: Second Division Champions, 1951/52. Team group featuring Eddie Gannon, Norman Curtis, Douglas Witcomb, Jack Marriott, Jack Sewell, Derek Dooley and Walter Rickett. The Owls finished top above Cardiff in a season dominated by new goalscoring sensation Derek Dooley, who claimed almost half of all Wednesday's goals. The Owls won promotion with exactly 100 goals and 46 of them came from Dooley. Not bad for someone who didn't get into the side until October! For the record, Jack Sewell finished as second-top scorer, chipping in with 23 goals. But the season belonged to Dooley and what a tragedy it was that it proved to be his last full campaign.

Opposite: The legendary Derek Dooley. A stocky, 6ft 2in centre-forward with size 12 feet, Dooley cut an imposing figure on the pitch and used his fearsome frame to 'charge' goalkeepers in the days when they received much less protection from match officials. A boyhood Wednesday fan, Dooley realised his dream of playing for the Owls in 1947 after playing as an amateur for Lincoln City. Following a slow start to his Wednesday career, he bagged his incredible haul of 47 goals in 31 League and cup games during the 1951/52 campaign.

Derek Dooley meets an effigy of himself on Rag Day (1 November) 1952.

NEWCASTLE UNITED
FOOTBALL CLUB
ST. JAMES' PARK
NEWCASTLE/TYNE
WINNERS OF F.A. CUP
1910,1924,1932,1951,1952
SEASON
1952-3
OFFICIAL PROGRAMME
PRICE 3D.
A. McMICHAEL
Newcastle United's Left Back.
Football League Division I.
NEWCASTLE UNITED
VERSUS
SHEFFIELD WED.
SATURDAY, 20th DEC., 1952.
Kick-off 2 p.m.
Programme No. 21

A programme from the game at Newcastle during the 1952/53 campaign. Wednesday enjoyed their best away win of the season at St James' Park, Derek Dooley and Jack Sewell grabbing two goals apiece in a 5-1 victory. Jack Marriott completed the scoring.

Signed from Chesterfield towards the end of the 1949/50 season, Hugh McJarrow immediately established himself as a first-team regular. He made a useful contribution, scoring 21 goals in 47 appearances, before moving to Luton in February 1952.

Above: Owls on the golf course, in the mid-1950s. Don McEvoy's drive is watched by (from left to right) Jack Marshall, Norman Curtis, Eric Taylor, Roy Shiner and Tom McAnearney.

Opposite above: Derek Dooley in action against Chelsea, November 1952. Also in the picture are Ron Greenwood and John Harris. Dooley's career was tragically ended just three months later. During a game at Preston in February 1953, he collided with North End keeper George Thompson as they raced for the ball and suffered a broken leg. The wound subsequently became infected and Dooley was told the harrowing news that the limb would have to be amputated to save his life. His record for Wednesday was a remarkable 63 goals from the same number of appearances.

Opposite below: An aerial view of Hillsborough, *c.* 1953.

Redfern Froggatt, whose father Frank starred for Wednesday in the 1920s, made over 500 appearances in twenty years at Hillsborough. He featured in four promotion-winning teams, captaining the 1958/59 Second Division Championship side. Froggatt was a fine inside-forward who may well have won more than his four England caps if Wednesday had enjoyed greater success during his time at the club. He retired in 1962.

Dr Andrew Stephen was appointed chairman of Wednesday in 1955, replacing Colonel Craig, who retired due to ill health. He became chairman of the FA in 1967, following in the illustrious footsteps of one of his predecessors at Hillsborough, Sir Charles Clegg.

Fans celebrating on the pitch after the final game of the season at home to Lincoln. After securing the Second Division title the previous week with a 5-2 win at Bury, Wednesday romped to a 5-3 victory over the Imps. Top scorer Roy Shiner grabbed a hat-trick, with Alan Finney scoring the other two.

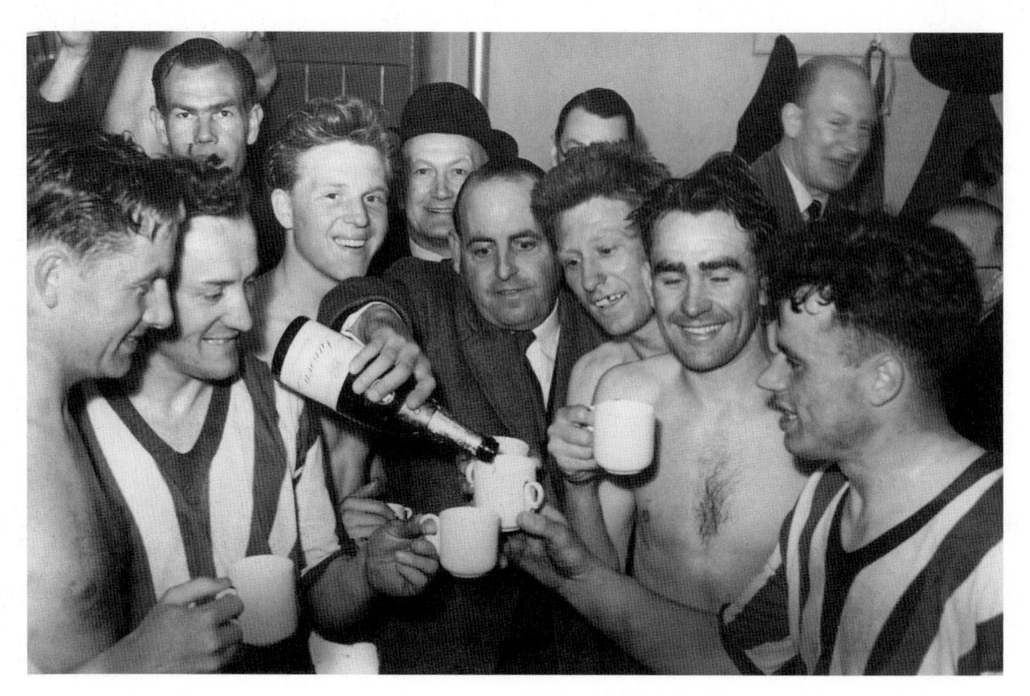

Eric Taylor pours the champagne as Wednesday celebrate winning the 1955/56 Second Division Championship. The players include David McIntosh, Redfern Froggatt, Norman Curtis, Albert Quixall, James McAnearney, Alan Finney and Don McEvoy. After finishing bottom of the First Division the previous season, Wednesday returned to the top-flight at the first attempt. They scored 101 goals with Roy Shiner notching 33 of them.

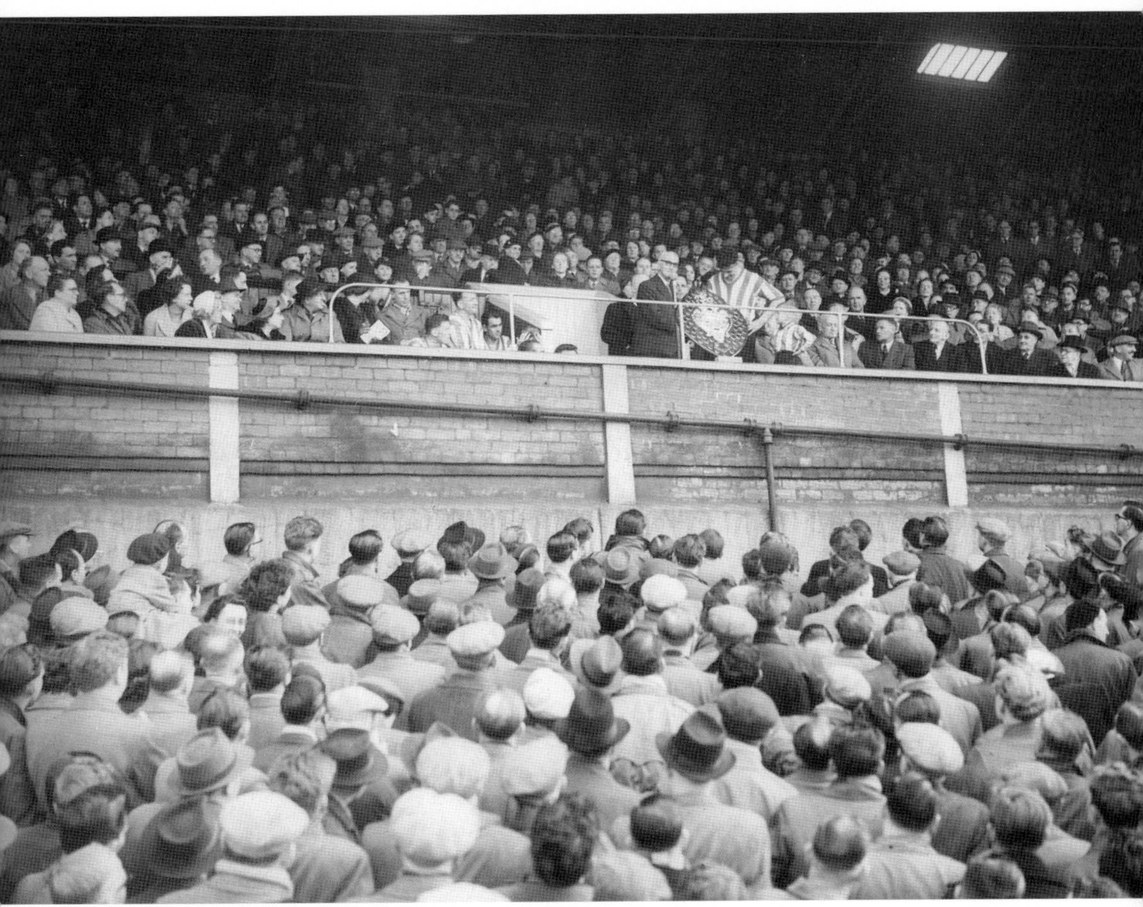

Don McEvoy receives the Second Division Championship shield. McEvoy cost £15,000 when he was signed from Huddersfield in 1954. Eric Taylor drafted him in to shore up a defence that had shipped 26 goals in seven games. He could not prevent Wednesday from being relegated, but the next season he skippered them back to the top-flight. After making 112 appearances, McEvoy joined Lincoln in 1958.

OFFICIAL
PROGRAMME

PRICE 3D.

SHEFFIELD FOOTBALL CLUB
CENTENARY

SHEFFIELD

versus

ENGLAND 'B'

WEDNESDAY, 23rd OCTOBER, 1957

Kick-off 7.15 p.m.

(BY FLOODLIGHT)

Left: The programme from the Sheffield *v.* England 'B' match during the 1957/58 season. The match was staged as part of Sheffield FC's centenary celebrations. The Sheffield line-up featured players from Rotherham, Barnsley and Doncaster as well as Wednesday and United. Wednesday were represented by Don Gibson, Don McEvoy, Alan Finney and Albert Quixall. Bobby Robson, who of course later managed the national side, was part of the England 'B' squad.

SHEFFIELD WEDNESDAY versus

JUVENTUS (Italy)

JOHN CHARLES
(Wales)
ENRICO SAVORI
(Argentine)
plus 9 Italian
internationals

THURSDAY
28th November, 1957
Kick-off 7.0 p.m.

The finest
footballing
combination
of the
present time

The Sheffield Wednesday Football Club does not guarantee that the proposed match will take place.

GANGWAY I

Reserved
Seat 5/-

Row | Seat

Above: Players line up before a 4-2 defeat at home to Arsenal on 22 September 1956. Albert Quixall scored both Wednesday goals. From left to right, back row: Tom McAnearney Ron Staniforth, Peter Swan, Dave McIntosh, Albert Broadbent, Ralph O'Donnell, Norman Curtis. Front row: Alan Finney, Albert Quixall, Roy Shiner, Dave Cargill.

Opposite below: Ticket for a friendly game against Juventus in November 1957. A crowd of nearly 45,000 saw an exciting match, with the Italian giants winning 4-3, Wales international John Charles scoring the winner.

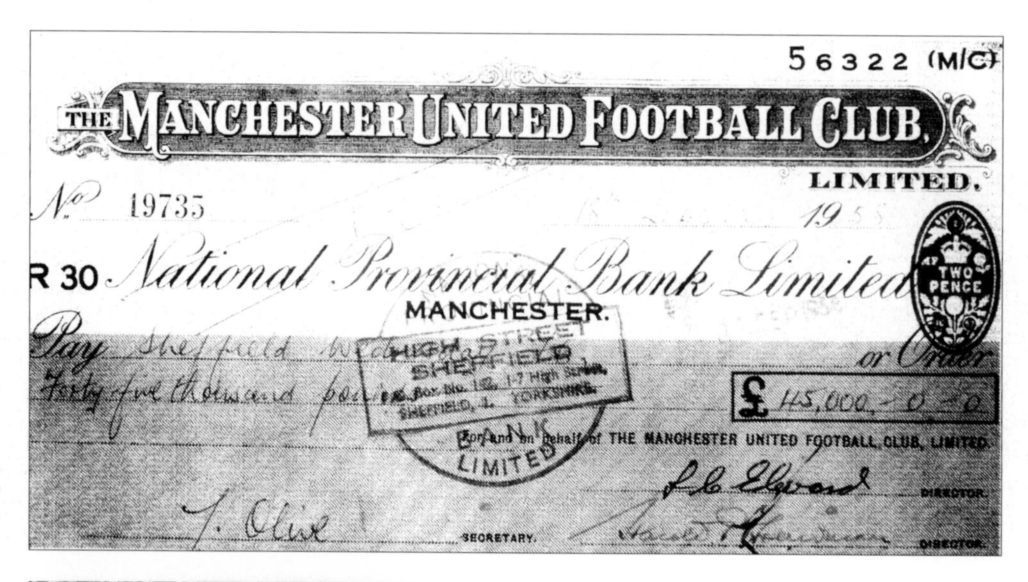

56322 (M/C)

THE MANCHESTER UNITED FOOTBALL CLUB, LIMITED.

No 19735 ... 195

R 30 National Provincial Bank Limited

MANCHESTER.

Pay Sheffield W... or Order

Forty five thousand pounds

£ 45,000-0-0

HIGH STREET SHEFFIELD

P.O. Box No. 12, 1-7 High Street, SHEFFIELD, 1. YORKSHIRE.

BANK LIMITED

TWO PENCE

For and on behalf of THE MANCHESTER UNITED FOOTBALL CLUB, LIMITED.

DIRECTOR.

SECRETARY.

DIRECTOR.

Above: 1958/59 squad with the Second Division Championship shield. The Owls sealed promotion with four games remaining. They went on to lift the title after thrashing South Yorkshire neighbours Barnsley 5-0 in their final home fixture, Redfern Froggatt and Roy Shiner scoring two goals apiece. Wednesday's title success owed much to their home form as they held off a challenge from Fulham, suffering just one defeat at Hillsborough.

Opposite above: The cheque received from Manchester United for Albert Quixall in 1958. The £45,000 fee was a British record as Matt Busby began the task of assembling a new side following the Munich Air Disaster. Quixall, who was a product of Wednesday's youth system, featured prominently in the 1951/52 and 1955/56 Second Division Championship sides. He scored 65 goals in 205 appearances for the Owls and won his five England caps while at Hillsborough.

Opposite below: Players walking during pre-season training, 1958. Wednesday were preparing for life back in Division Two after suffering relegation for the third time in a decade that saw them earn a reputation as a 'yo-yo' team. The board initiated a managerial shake-up in a bid to reverse the trend. Eric Taylor switched to the role of secretary, with the manager's job advertised for the first time since the 1930s. Tottenham's assistant manager Bill Nicholson, who went on to lead Spurs to the double in 1961, was interviewed, but the decision was taken to poach Harry Catterick from Rochdale, just nine days before the big kick-off.

Peter Swan emerged as an influential figure for Wednesday in the early 1960s after signing as an amateur in 1952. He took over from Don McEvoy in central defence in 1958 and helped Wednesday win the Second Division title the following year. With 19 full England caps to his name, Swan appeared set for a long and successful career in the game. But along with David Layne (who had moved to Everton) and Tony Kay he was handed a life ban in 1964 following a betting scandal which rocked the club. The trio were found guilty of backing Ipswich to beat Wednesday in a match they were involved in. The suspension was lifted eight years later and Swan returned to Wednesday, but he made just 17 appearances before being transferred to Bury. Had it not been for his enforced absence, Swan may well have played in England's 1966 World Cup-winning side.

England keeper Ron Springett enjoyed a nine-year spell at Hillsborough after signing from QPR towards the end of the 1957/58 season. He soon established himself as Wednesday's first-choice shot-stopper but was unable to prevent them being relegated from the top flight. But Springett played a key role in the Second Division title success the following year and featured prominently under Harry Catterick and his successors Vic Buckingham and Alan Brown. After turning out 384 times for Wednesday, Springett returned to QPR in 1967 in a part-exchange deal involving his younger brother Peter. Ron was valued at £16,000 in the transfer while Peter cost £40,000. Peter Springett went on to make 207 appearances in eight years at Hillsborough before joining Barnsley on a free transfer.

Ron Springett's first England cap. He won 33 in total.

1960/61 team group. From left to right, back row: Johnny Quinn, Peter Johnson, Gerry Young, Peter Swan, Ron Springett, Tom McAnearney, Don Megson, Tony Kay. Front row: Derek Wilkinson, Bobby Craig, Keith Ellis, Alan Finney (captain), Harry Catterick (manager), John Fantham, Billy Griffin. In this season, Wednesday were First Division runners-up and FA Cup quarter-finalists. The likes of Tony Kay, Peter Swan and John Fantham flourished under Harry Catterick, who quit suddenly in 1961. It is generally believed he was unhappy with the lack of cash available for signings and did not enjoy a good working relationship with Eric Taylor. An offer to return to Goodison Park also proved impossible for the former Everton centre-forward to turn down.

Eric Taylor and Harold Jessop pictured during the four-match tour of Nigeria in 1960. The locals had a liking for invading the pitch and there was a mini-riot during a highly-charged game against East Nigeria!

Opposite above: Vic Buckingham with Eric Taylor. Buckingham was named as Harry Catterick's successor in May 1961. The flamboyant Londoner had led Dutch giants Ajax to League and cup success and hopes were high that his arrival would herald the start of a bright new era at Hillsborough. But Buckingham failed to deliver any silverware and his contract was not renewed when it expired in the spring of 1964. In retrospect, Buckingham's record appears quite good, especially when Wednesday's decline in the late 1960s is taken into account. The Owls achieved a top-six finish in Division One in each of his three seasons and also reached the quarter-finals of the Fairs Cup.

Opposite below: Derek Dooley featured on the popular *This Is Your Life* television programme in 1961. The famous red book presented by Eammon Andrews is on display in a cabinet at Hillsborough's Dooleys Restaurant.

Both intelligently confused.

Keith Ellis bundles the ball home in a 2-0 win at Leyton Orient in 1961. The Sheffield-born centre-forward came through the ranks at Hillsborough, but it was several years before he managed to hold down a regular first-team place. He eventually established himself in the side under Harry Catterick and enjoyed his best spell in the 1960/61 season when he scored 19 goals in 37 appearances including a hat-trick in a 7-2 FA Cup win over Manchester United at Old Trafford. Ellis found himself back in the reserves when Vic Buckingham took charge and he was sold to Scunthorpe for £10,000 in 1964 after scoring 60 goals in 118 appearances.

Sir Stanley Rous, secretary of the FA, opens the new North Stand before the game against Bolton on 23 August 1961. The stand cost £150,000 to construct.

In his early days at the club, Billy Griffin was known as 'Billy the goal kid', earning his nickname with six goals in as many appearances in the 1959/60 season. However, he failed to win a regular place in the side and moved to Bury in 1962. His Wednesday record was 20 goals in 36 games.

David 'Bronco' Layne hailed from Sheffield, but he only joined Wednesday after spells at Rotherham, Swindon and Bradford. His impressive strike-rate convinced Vic Buckingham to sign him in 1962 and he proved to be a big hit, scoring 58 goals in 81 appearances before being banned in 1964. Like Peter Swan, Layne was invited to return to Hillsborough when his suspension was lifted in 1972, but he struggled following such a lengthy absence and left to join Hereford later that year after failing to force his way into the first-team.

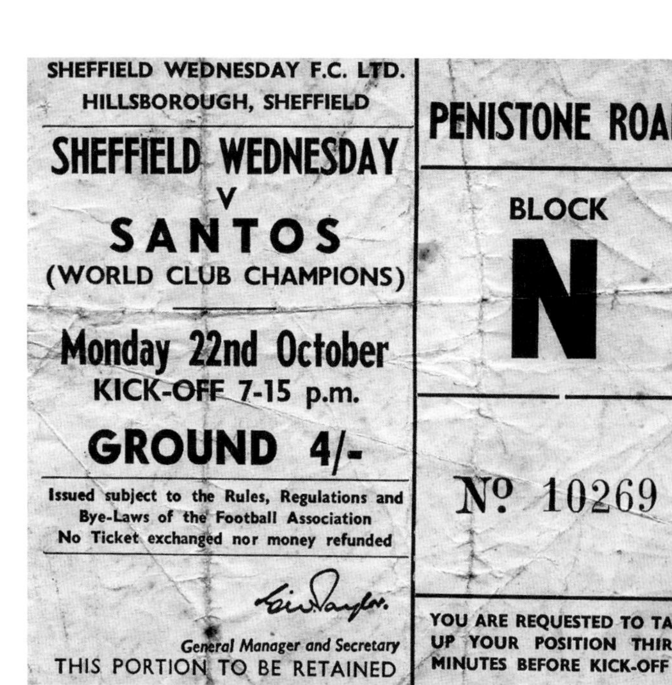

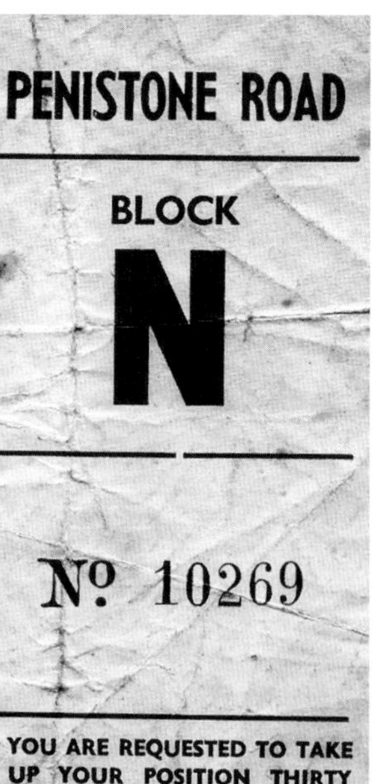

A ticket for the friendly match against Brazilian side Santos in 1962. The South Americans arrived at Hillsborough as reigning World Champions after beating Benfica over two legs. They included a twenty-one-year-old Pele in their side and were visiting Europe for the first time. The game attracted nearly 50,000 fans who witnessed a sublime performance from Santos. Billy Griffin and Bronco Layne scored Wednesday's goals in a 4-2 defeat.

Wednesday raided South Yorkshire neighbours Rotherham to sign Peter Johnson in 1957. He mainly played at full-back but also turned out on occasion as an emergency centre-forward. Johnson was ever-present when the Owls finished First Division runners-up in the 1960/61 season. He was also a fixture in the side during the following two seasons before losing his place to Brian Hill. After making 207 appearances, Johnson signed for Peterborough in 1965.

Programme from the Fairs Cup match at home to Barcelona in 1962. It was Wednesday's first European campaign and after beating Olympique Lyonnais and AS Roma, they faced the mighty Barcelona in the quarter-finals of the competition. The Owls won 3-2 in the first leg, but were knocked out after losing 2-0 in the return match watched by a crowd of 75,000.

Colin Dobson, who featured either as an inside-forward or winger, joined Wednesday as an amateur in the mid-1950s, but his insistence on completing his shipbuilding apprenticeship meant he did not turn professional until 1961. It was not long before Dobson earned a regular place, and he was capped by England at Under-23 level in 1963. After being overlooked towards the end of the 1965/66 season, he switched to Huddersfield. Dobson scored 52 goals in 193 appearances for the Owls.

Alan Brown, who succeeded Vic Buckingham in 1964, had a reputation as a tough disciplinarian. He was no stranger to Hillsborough, having been on the club's coaching staff in the early 1950s. There was much hope that Brown would revive Wednesday's fortunes when he led them to the FA Cup final in 1966, but that failed to happen and they were on a downward spiral when he quit to rejoin Sunderland in 1968.

An Agreement made the Twenty-second day of June 19 64 between ERIC WOODHOUSE TAYLOR of Hillsborough Sheffield 6 in the County of York the Secretary of and acting pursuant to Resolution and Authority for and on behalf of the SHEFFIELD WEDNESDAY FOOTBALL CLUB of Hillsborough Sheffield 6 (hereinafter referred to as the Club) of the one part and

DONALD HARRY MEGSON

of 10 Butler Road, Sheffield

in the County of Yorkshire Professional Football Player (hereinafter referred to as the Player) of the other part **Whereby** it is agreed as follows:—

1. The Player hereby agrees to play in an efficient manner and to the best of his ability for the Club for the period of one (year/~~years~~) (hereinafter called "the initial period of employment") from the First day of July to the 30th day of June 1965 Unless the initial period of employment shall either be (a) previously determined in accordance with the provisions of one or other of Clauses 10, 11, 12 or 13 hereof or (b) terminated extended or renewed as provided by Clauses 18 and 19 of this Agreement.

2. The Player shall attend the Club's ground or any other place decided upon by the Club for the purposes of or in connection with his training as a Player pursuant to the instructions of the Secretary, Manager, or Trainer of the Club, or of such other person, or persons as the Club may appoint. (This provision shall not apply if the Player is engaged by the Club at a weekly wage of less than One Pound or at a wage per match.)

3. The Player shall do everything necessary to get and keep himself in the best possible condition so as to render the most efficient service to the Club, and will carry out all the training and other instructions of the Club through its representative officials.

4. The Player shall observe and be subject to all the Rules, Regulations and Bye-Laws of the Football Association, and any other Association, League, or Combination of which the Club shall be a member. And this Agreement shall be subject to any action which shall be taken by The Football Association under their Rules for the suspension or termination of the Football Season, and if any such suspension or termination shall be decided upon the payment of wages shall likewise be suspended or terminated, as the case may be and in any proceedings by the Player against the Club it shall be a sufficient and complete defence and answer by and on the part of the Club that such suspension or termination hereof is due to the action of The Football Association, or any Sub-Committee thereof to whom the power may be delegated.

5. The Player shall not engage in any business or live in any place which the Directors (or Committee) of the Club may deem unsuitable.

6. Unless this Agreement has previously been determined by any one of Clauses 10, 11, 12 or 13 hereof as hereinafter provided, the Player shall not before the last day of the playing season next preceding the expiration of any further or additional further period for which this Agreement shall have been renewed in accordance with the provisions of Clauses 18 or 19 hereof or before the last day of the playing

Don Megson's contract in 1964.
The agreement was to pay Megson £25 per week with a signing-on fee of £260 per annum payable in two parts. Signed from non-League Mossley in 1952, Megson settled into the left-back role after being used in various positions. He had to wait seven years to make his League debut, but soon cemented his place in the side and won may admirers with his pace and whole-hearted commitment. Megson went on to skipper the side, taking over the captain's armband from Tom McAnearney. After notching up 442 appearances, he brought the curtain down on his eighteen-year career at Hillsborough in 1970 to become manager of Bristol Rovers.

Right: Sheffielder John Fantham turned professional in 1956 and made his League debut two years later. He shone in the early 1960s and won his solitary full England cap in 1961. Fantham overtook Redfern Froggatt as Wednesday's record post-war goalscorer in 1968. But just a year later, Danny Williams decided to sell him to Rotherham for £5,000. Fantham's record for the Owls was an impressive 167 goals in 435 appearances.

Below: Mark Pearson (left) and Gerry Young in 1964. Sheffield-born Pearson began his career at Manchester United and made his debut against Wednesday at Old Trafford in the first game after the Munich Air Disaster. Nicknamed 'Pancho' because of his Mexican-style sideburns, Pearson signed for the Owls in 1963. Expectations were high, but he failed to make a real impact and his Wednesday career effectively ended after he broke the same leg twice during the 1964/65 season. After scoring nine goals in 40 games, Pearson was allowed to join Fulham in the summer of 1965.

John Quinn developed a reputation for versatility after starting out as an inside-forward. He was happy to play wherever he was required and commanded respect from his team-mates. Quinn was signed from Prescot Cables in 1959, but it was several years before he held down a regular place in the side. After finding himself on the fringes of the first team, Quinn made the short move to Rotherham in 1967. He was just five games short of 200 appearances for the Owls.

David Ford is among the select band of players to have played for both Sheffield clubs. He started out with Wednesday and became the first substitute to be used by the Owls in a League match when he made his debut against Sunderland in October 1965. Ford showed much promise as an inside-forward, winning England Under-23 caps, before tragedy struck in 1967. He was involved in a serious car accident which claimed the life of his fiancée and it took him a long time to make a full recovery. After scoring 37 goals in 135 appearances, Ford left to join Newcastle in 1969. He signed for Sheffield United just over a year later.

1965 team group. From left to right, back row: Peter Eustace, Brian Hill, John Hickton, Ron Springett, Vic Mobley, Don Megson, John Quinn. Front row: Wilf Smith, Colin Dobson, Brian Usher, John Fantham, Alan Finney, Gerry Young. This new-look kit was something of a break with tradition.

An unusual picture of the players and staff from 1966. Incidentally, the introduction of a kit without the traditional blue and white stripes in the summer of 1965 upset many supporters. But the blue shirts with white sleeves lasted for seven years until the stripes returned.

Left: 1966 FA Cup final programme. After seeing off Reading, Newcastle, Huddersfield and Blackburn, the Owls faced a semi-final tie Chelsea at Villa Park. Goals from Jim McCalliog and Graham Pugh gave Alan Brown's men a 2-0 win in front of a crowd of 61,321 to set up a clash with Everton in the final.

Below: Eric Taylor with Eamonn Andrews before the cup final.

FRIDAY	13th May	SATURDAY	14th May
			Breakfast up to 10.30.
13.25	Assemble Midland Station.	11.20	Assemble in the Main Lounge.
13.55	Depart for London (Pullman Reserved seats) Afternoon tea en route.	11.30	Depart by Motor Coaches for Wembley. Sandwich Lunch en route.
17.03	Arrive St. Pancras Station. Motor Coaches to convey party to Headquarters: Hotel Russell, Russell Square, London, W.C.1. Tel. No. Terminus 6470		**YOUR COACH IS No. 4**
	YOUR COACH IS No. 4	13.30	E.T.A. Wembley Stadium.
		15.00	Kick off.
		17.15	Motor Coaches leave the Stadium for H.Q.
	Evening free.	19.30	Reception for Banquet at Hotel Russell (Wharncliffe Suite).

The 1966 FA Cup final itinerary. Wednesday experienced a disappointing League campaign, finishing seventeenth in Division One, but they gave themselves a chance of lifting some silverware by making their first FA Cup final appearance in thirty-one years.

David Ford follows up to turn the ball home after John Fantham's shot has been parried by Gordon West, to give Wednesday a 2-0 lead in the 1935 FA Cup final. Jim McCalliog had opened the scoring in the fourth minute. But Everton hit back strongly to win 3-2 with goals from Trebilcock (2) and Temple.

Sheffield Wednesday
Football Club

Banquet

Alphabetical List of Guests
and Seating Arrangements

Hotel Russell, London

Saturday, 14th May, 1966

Left: Menu for the FA Cup banquet. The result at Wembley was harsh on a youthful Wednesday side who played their part in a highly entertaining final. Their performance was recognised by the supporters who turned out to give them a warm welcome when they returned to Sheffield.

Below: Wednesday embarked on a three-week, six-match tour of the Far East in the summer of 1966. They faced Fulham three times, playing the other games against local teams.

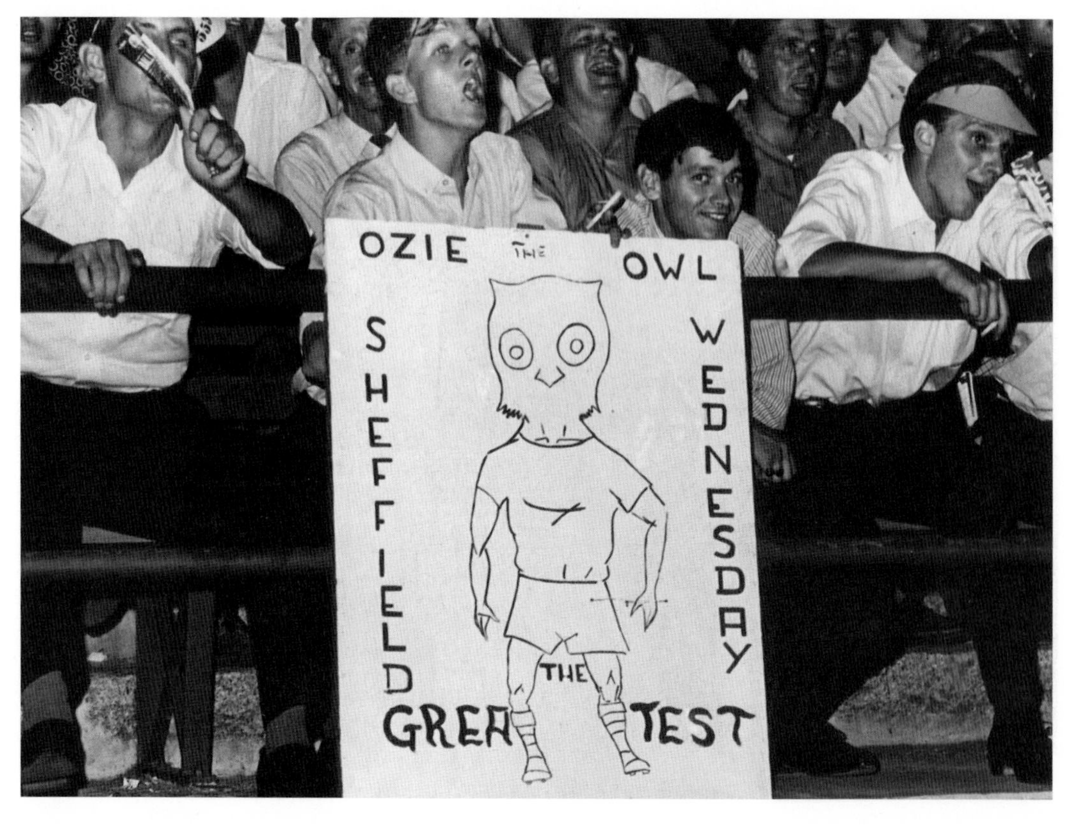

A new 4,471-seater stand at the Leppings Lane end was constructed in time for the 1966 World Cup games played at Hillsborough. The structure, which also included a terraced area, cost £109,036 to build. It was first used for the Switzerland *v.* Germany match on 12 July 1966.

A view of Hillsborough taken before the World Cup games.

An electronic scoreboard was installed on the Kop in time for the World Cup games staged at Hillsborough. It kept fans informed of scores from the other World Cup matches being played. The scoreboard remained in use until falling into disrepair in the mid-1970s.

Action from the West Germany *v.* Uruguay World Cup quarter-final at Hillsborough on 23 July 1966. Uruguay had two players sent off in a stormy match and lost 4-0 in front of a crowd of 40,007.

Players training at Lilleshall before an FA Cup tie in 1967.

Celebrations in Wednesday's centenary year were low-key. In typical Sheffield fashion, little fuss was made at reaching the milestone. Fortunately, someone had the foresight to bake a cake to mark the club's 100th birthday!

Acknowledgements

I would first of all like to thank James Howarth at Tempus Publishing for asking me to write this book as well as providing help and guidance when required. Thanks also to editors Rob Sharman and Fran Gannon.

I wish to thank Sheffield Wednesday FC for providing photographs and memorabilia. I am indebted to chairman Dave Allen for granting me unrestricted access to the club's archives. Thanks also to communications manager Steve Chu and his colleagues Francis Hall and Mark Brailsford for their assistance in assembling the items. Wednesday historian Jason Dickinson also deserves praise for his help in locating the material and providing information on players.

John Higginbotham, Andy Parsisson and Ian Pearson assisted the project by loaning photographs and other items from their personal collections following a plea in the *Sheffield Star*'s 'Diary' column, compiled by Martin Dawes, which sparked a tremendous response. John got in touch to offer a collection of around 100 photographs from the personal collection of former Owls keeper Ted Davison.

A binman friend of John's rescued the pictures – valued at around £5,000 – which had apparently been thrown out with the household rubbish after Davison passed away.

Thanks also to Doug Hindmarch at Sheffield Central Library, Leon Rothman and Malcolm 'Chalky' White for assisting my research.

I spent many hours scanning the various images at JMC in Tibshelf, Derbyshire and thanks go to my brother Mark and designer Vicky Oakton for their invaluable help. Chris Sanders at Bonds Gallery in Chesterfield also helped with the process of dealing with framed pictures.

On a personal note, my parents William and Sheila continue to offer their valued support and encouragement in my career. My father, a keen historian, also provided valuable background information on the Clegg brothers, Sir Charles and Sir William, who are related to my family.

I should also thank Carolyn Dennis for nagging, sorry, prompting me to get on with the project when my momentum waned!